MY STORY

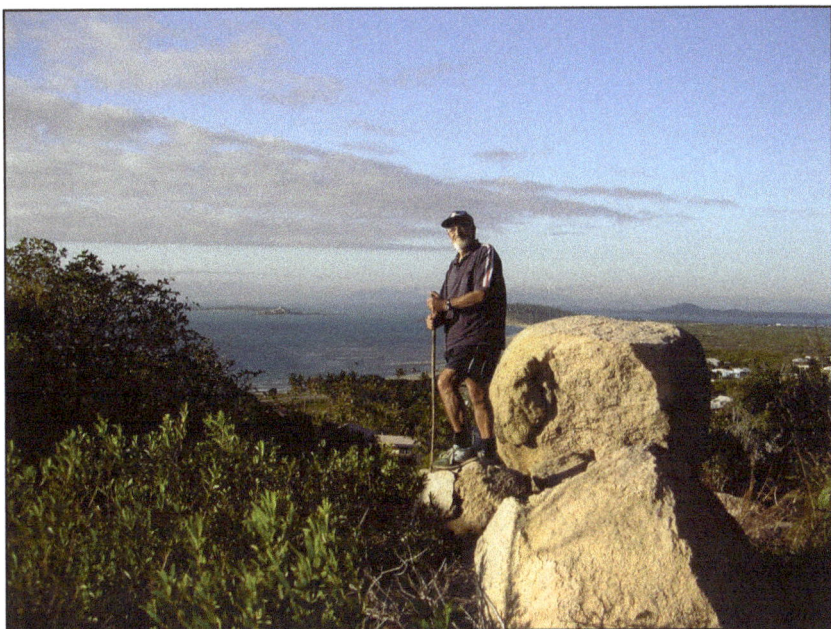

Bruce D. Prewer

Ideas into Books®
WESTVIEW
Kingston Springs, Tennessee USA

Ideas into Books®
W E S T V I E W
P.O. Box 605
Kingston Springs, TN 37082
www.publishedbywestview.com

ISBN 978-1-62880-026-5

Second edition, Easter 2018

Digitally printed on acid free paper.

Foreword

The first, limited edition of this volume, *My Story*, came as an utter surprise to me. I had no direct hand in it; nor did my wife Marie Joyce; none; zilch!

On the morning of our sixtieth wedding anniversary, our dear friend Helen Hall, who for the last few years has been my proofreader/secretary (gratis), popped in to our home with a gorgeous sheath of roses. Then from a voluminous carry bag Helen produced two wrapped copies of a book. We opened our parcels and were gob-smacked! It was *My Story,* a most generous, personal gift from our special USA friend and publisher Mary Nelson.

Mary for over six months had been plotting with Helen, and with the connivance of our family, produced this volume. Sourced by a personal story-line I had shared with Mary and with letters I had written a few years ago to our eight grandchildren, plus photographs from various family albums, Mary put together *My Story* much as it is here presented in this second edition.

Bruce D Prewer

March 3, 2018

Some Childhood Memories

1932-1949

Bruce David Prewer

FROM CRADLE TO 18TH YEAR

Early Memories

Bruce David was born to Florrie and Cliff Prewer in Launceston, Tasmania, on 28th April 1931, the youngest of four children: Margaret, Raymond, followed a decade later, by Dorothy and Bruce. My dad was a shy, hardworking, sombre man, my mother a cheerful, outgoing and generous woman.

My earliest memories arise from when I was a little child under the age of four years, living on a small dairy farm just a couple of miles out of Launceston. Three memories stand out: the warmth of waking up in the cot in my parents' bedroom and feeling loved, being swooped on by spur-winged plovers while pulling a red toy on string across a small paddock and finding out something horrible about my dad.

The last of these three sharp memories needs some further comment. Dorothy, two years older than I, led me into some nearby bushland to show me a shallow pit filled with the rotting carcasses of young calves. She told me that whenever little bull calves were born, Dad took them into this smelly hole and hit them on the head with the back of an axe. This was my first meeting with death. It shook me to the very core of my little being. What made it worse, when had I once asked my father where the infant bull calves disappeared to shortly after they were born, was that he had told me God took them back to heaven.

Although I thought our father loved us, what he did to the calves, and then fibbed about it, made me wary of ever completely trusting him again.

Moving House

Shortly before my fourth birthday, we shifted house to a larger dairy farm at Dilston, nine miles from Launceston. Most of the rest of my childhood was spent in that (then) mainly apple-growing region in the Tamar River Valley. Our convict-built house was set on a beautiful site overlooking the main road and the Tamar River. Many seagoing ships of that era came and went past our house to the Port of Launceston, including the largish Bass Strait passenger ferry, the *SS Taroona*.

Apart from my sister Dot, there were no other children living nearby. My main playmate was my dog, Nip. In Nip's company I roamed every corner of the farm and the bushland we owned. From my early days I was deeply affected by nature: the various trees and flowering bushes, the magpies and native hens and the wedge-tailed eagles with a wingspan of six to eight feet. I knew the nesting places of swallows, the colours of various birds' eggs, where to find native mushrooms, and I often visited the tree ferns, maiden hair fern, tiny native violets and mosses that were prolific in a special patch of dense rainforest near the riverbank. From an early age I sensed a Spirit-Something in the wild for which no one seemed to have a name.

We were exceedingly poor. I mean, really poor. But there was always plenty of wholesome, home-grown food. My clothes, though much patched, were kept clean and tidy. Best of all I felt loved, mostly by my mum and my big sister Margaret who tended to spoil her little brother.

Good Church

On Sunday mornings Dad drove us to a small weatherboard Methodist church at a place aptly called Swan Bay. Hundreds of black swans would frequent the bay's shallow waters. Apart from the boring music (the organist could only play music for about 10 hymns from a red-covered *Sankey's* hymn book) I rather liked that morning church. The service was often led by a jovial minister named Charles Gallagher, who treated us kids like real people.

After church, while the adults chatted on matters farming outside in the sunshine, we children played on the beach, looking for shells, skimming smooth pebbles across the water and watching the hosts of swans feeding upside down.

Yes, that church experience was… you know… ok.

Bad Church

Sunday afternoons were a different story. Mum and Dad had a sleep on Sunday afternoons (or so they claimed!) while Dorothy and I were packed off at 2pm to Sunday School, held in the Dilston Hall. Miss James was our teacher. A kindly spinster, she had us learn by rote many Bible texts, and told us Bible stories. Some of the stories were a bit frightening – like that one where Abraham took his only son and was about to sacrifice him on an altar, until God stopped him. There was a coloured picture in Miss James' story book, showing Abraham standing over the terrified child with a large, curved, wicked knife. That was nightmare stuff. My dad would never do that… or… would he? After all, he did kill those little baby bulls with the back of an axe!

Our parents insisted that Dorothy and I stay on for the church service that followed at 3pm. Sheer terror. Led by 'evangelists' (yuk) from the Gospel Hall in Launceston, religious bullies of the first order, they shouted at or pleaded with us to convert to God and appease his anger, warning of the fires of hell and the unending nature of torture throughout eternity. It was utter child abuse and scarred me with a deep-seated anxiety.

Yet I refused to publicly cower to these violent preachers. I vowed that they would never make me convert to such an abominable God. I was scared witless that they might be right, but I would not submit. The fact that they mixed up that lovely Jesus (whom we heard about at Swan Bay) with their vicious

God, left me confused. How could Bad God and Jesus belong together?

You might ask why didn't our parents stop this abuse? Whenever Dorothy and I complained, they thought we were typical kids, exaggerating to try and get out of some good, Christian discipline. We tried wagging it once but were found hiding in the maize crop and were severely punished.

Bad Sex

I attended the one-room, one-teacher school at Dilston. Just 25 kids were enrolled. I was the youngest kid in the school. In my second year, the older kids got into sexual exploration. One lunch hour, behind the shelter-shed, two 14-year-old girls asked to look at my dicky. Then they pulled down their panties and rubbed my dicky on their mickies. They warned me never to tell anyone, or I would get into big trouble. Sex must be bad stuff? After that, I experienced times of arousal that I doubt were normal for a six-year-old child.

Worse was to follow. On a freezing, rainy morning in early winter, three police arrived and ordered all the pupils outside to the shelter-shed. Starting with the oldest, one by one they called out a child's name to go back inside the classroom. When they finished with each pupil, they would be sent straight home, not allowed to speak with the remainder of us as we huddled in the shelter-shed. It was a long, anxiety-ridden wait, especially for us younger ones.

At 5pm I was the last one left, alone and shivering in the shed. Then my name was called. The police made me stand up straight in front of a table while they interrogated me. The tall and very fat sergeant asked many questions; very particularly about Veronica, a grade six girl who one day was chased into the toilet by a big boy named Farmer. I kept to myself the secret of what happened with the two senior girls and me. It seemed to me that sex must be worse than bad; it was criminal and very, very wicked.

Good hospital

When I was 11 years old, I spent three months in the Launceston General Hospital recovering from rheumatic fever. I was terrified, and acutely shy at first, yet it became one of the best experiences of my childhood. I gained a lot in confidence, met many different people, discovered the world of comics and National Geographic, and had a crush on some nurses.

My specialist medico was a very strict young doctor, who enforced complete (I mean total!) bed rest for eight weeks. I am the only person I know from that era (prior to modern antibiotics) who recovered from that disease without carrying permanent heart damage.

Things are a-changing

In the year I turned 12, we moved to the outskirts of Launceston, a quiet, semi-rural area called Alanvale. Dad sold the Dilston farm and returned to work with a builder he'd first worked with 20 years before.

I sat for an exam called the Ability Test and was one of the lucky 10% who gained access to secondary schooling. I attended the Launceston Technical College. These were four years of becoming a town kid, making good mates, getting into minor scrapes, thinking and talking a lot about girls, developing a keen interest in the English language, becoming the editor of the school magazine and finally leaving school not knowing what I wanted to do with my life.

One bad experience of this period was being sexually assaulted by a tattooed man in a public toilet. It left me feeling very dirty – I showered excessively that day and through the following weeks.

God and the church

While still at school, I and my best mate Terry decided we were atheists and made it our business to make the weekly class of Religious Instruction a purgatory for the visiting minister.

Strangely, I still kept attending church, at the Methodist church in the suburb of Invermay. What kept me attending? Good mates attended that church, plus we had some lovely girls to ogle or flirt with. A second factor was the music. For the first time in my life, I discovered great congregational singing and the stirring music of a pipe organ. The Methodist Hymn Book was a revelation; notably the poetry and music set to some of its 984 songs. I became a member of the men's choir.

My addiction to using foul language, my cowardice when other kids were bullied at school, my dishonesty to my parents and my almost daily cruel teasing of my sister Dorothy, made me wonder what I would in fact make of my life. All my good New Year's resolutions quickly fell in a heap.

Publicly I wore a cheerful face. Privately I became very introspective and discontented with myself. A Bible passage in one of Paul's writings summed me up; *"The good that I would I do not, and that which I would not do, that I do. Who can rescue me?"* I knew the answer wasn't in myself, but that word 'God', which most people seemed to have no problem with, for me still carried all the negative baggage of those preacher-bullies who made my life so miserable at Dilston church. There was no way I would find an answer to my personal inner chaos in that religious stuff!

Surprise, surprise!

By 1949, I was working in the very stuffy atmosphere of the ES&A Bank (English, Scottish & Australian Bank Limited). After three months, I knew banking was not my scene.

In late February that year, I went reluctantly with some church friends to hear a visiting preacher. I don't remember much of the sermon, except his insistent call to give one's life to Jesus. Jesus I could dig, but not God, so I gave all I understood of myself, to all I understood of Jesus. My whole being began to sing. With two of my mates, Wilfred and Peter, I went forward afterwards for some counselling.

I returned home that night filled with some Presence I did not understand. My dear, overjoyed mother said it was the Spirit of God. Well, I found this new Spirit-thing to be a warm, loving companion. My faith at this stage was lopsided, but that did not bother me at all. My whole world had become new. What was more, now I seemed to have more control of my words and deeds. I continued to work at the bank and the boring stuff did not seem as intolerable as it had before.

A new minister

L ate that April, a new minister was inducted during the service of the church that I now eagerly attended. I found him to be a robust character with a robust faith. He and his wife had a young son and two daughters. The eldest was a dark-haired, slender-waisted 18-year-old.

I was glad to be asked to escort the 18-year-old on her first outing with our church youth group. I found her cheerful chatter, her much wider experience than mine and a dare-devil streak in her attitude, to be most captivating. She had lived in the tropics and England, had circumnavigated the world, had studied at an elite girls' school in Melbourne and was right then commencing training to be a nursing sister.

Before many weeks had passed, I was proud to be able to call her my girlfriend. She was not like other girls I'd known; she was not a typical, compliant woman (as most were expected to be in those days) nor was she mainly interested in frills, make-up and perfume. She had a mind and an opinion of her own and was not slow to make it known. Early in our time together, she declared that she would never marry a minister. It didn't worry me at all. I had no thoughts in that direction.

A spanner in the works

Slowly I was sorting out where God (the God of Jesus, not the bullying abomination of my childhood) fitted into my developing faith, but before long this God of Jesus burst apart all my pretty new plans for my future.

It happened this way. One Sunday evening, as I sat with the men's choir at our church, a Voice so soft that no one else could possibly hear it, yet so voluminous that it blotted out all other thoughts in my head, said simply, *"Bruce, I want you to be my minister."*

I was shocked and shaken. An internal protest raged within me. *No way. You've got the wrong man. I could never be a minister. I have done no public speaking. I get tongue tied when I stand up in front of people. Not educated enough. I don't have any of the necessary gifts. No can do. You will have to look elsewhere. Besides, let's cut to the chase – my lovely girlfriend will ditch me if I agree!*

Such internal dialogue went on throughout three days. Then I gave in: *If you, God, can in any way use me, you're welcome. The one likely gift I might have for ministry is that of being a good listener. If that will do you, so be it. But I still reckon you have called the wrong bloke.*

The biggest decision of my life was now made. Even though it meant losing my lovely, feisty girlfriend, I would go ahead with what God wanted.

Marie at 18 years, 3 months after we met.

11 years old, with my dog 'Nip'

17.9 yrs, on front veranda steps, Alanvale.

18.7 yrs, after taking service at Georgetown.

PREPARING FOR MINISTRY: 1950~1954

The bridge had been crossed and was burnt behind me. I agreed to allow the Holy Spirit to make a minister out of me. If She could, that is.

Plucked up my courage and told my girlfriend, who *would never marry a minister*, of my intentions. She was not exactly delighted with my news. She looked down for a few moments, absorbing the implications. Then this surprising young woman reached for my hand, looked shyly into my eyes and said: "If that's what we must do, ok, let's do it." I loved that '*we*'! I really wanted to spend the rest of my life with this Marie Joyce Goldsmith.

Later that week I talked with her father, George Goldsmith, about my unexpected call to the ministry of the church. He did not frown at my presumption or even look surprised; gave me nothing but warm, thoughtful encouragement. When I talked of the handicap of my shyness, he said the good Lord would take care of that. After praying with me, he suggested I talk to Rev. Ern Baker, the executive secretary for the Tasmania region of the Methodist Church, who was the contact person for the Home Mission Training College, at 'Otira' in Kew, Melbourne.

This formidable character, Rev. Ern Baker, quizzed me; he did not seem impressed by my primitive understanding of the faith and the church. However, trusting the judgement of G.T. Goldsmith, he agreed to put my name to the Rev. Alex Pederick, who was the Principal of Otira Training College. In the meantime, he suggested I began taking small parts in worship and, maybe, try preaching a sermon in some of the smaller country churches.

My first attempt at preaching was in the small, weatherboard church at Swan Bay on the Tamar River; the place where for some years my family had worshipped during my childhood. I was given transport by a qualified lay preacher, called Mr. Maynard, who was the manager of ANA (Australian National Airways) in Launceston. The first sermon was on the subject of 'The Peace of Christ', delivered breathlessly to the background music of black swans honking on the shallow feeding grounds of the bay. Evidently Mr. Maynard, a kindly soul, gave a positive report, because I was allowed to lead some more services around the 'Invermay Circuit' of the Methodist Church.

The 'big one' came when I was asked to preach at a youth service at the chief church, Invermay. This demanded a public witness to my faith in my home church, in the presence of some of those callow youths with whom I used to sit in the back seat and make snide remarks. Anxiety soared up to level nine! With my stomach in turmoil and sweating plentifully, I managed to deliver my second sermon.

At the end of January 1950, I left home for good. On the way to the airport, we called at my sister Margaret's house at Mowbray (she had an infected foot) and kissed her goodbye on the front steps. I had no clue or premonition of the crisis that would shortly engulf her. From the airport at Western Junction I took my first ever flight with ANA, and with my eyes out on stalks as I took in the magnitude and bustle of Melbourne, I had myself delivered by taxi from Essendon Airport to 59 Walpole Street, Kew.

With a handful of other young Home Mission trainees, I soon felt at home within the close-knit fellowship of Otira, under the sometimes-bossy care of Matron Ross and the benevolent dictatorship of the Rev. Alec Pederick. I was not the youngest student. My new friend Bruce Rollins (from Geelong) held that honour by a few months. Some of the other fellows, like the warm hearted former industrial chemist Brian Smith, seemed wonderfully sophisticated at the mature age of 26 years.

Each day began with prayers in the Chapel, led by the Principal whom we came to love as *Peddo*. The week was taken up with lectures in Bible, theology, church history, Methodist law and church practice, and each Friday there was the dreaded preaching class. One student was rostered each week to lead worship and preach, under the oversight of the redoubtable older minister, the Rev. Norman Higgs. This was tough love in action. Each of us would emerge from our post-service session with our supervisor, utterly shaken. How could we make so many elementary mistakes? Wasn't the Holy Spirit meant to "lead us into all truth"? Were we really cut out to be preachers?

Evidently we just might be. Each weekend we were still rostered to lead worship in small towns across Victoria, circuits that were at that time without any minister or Home Missionary. My first experience was in Tallangatta, the old town, now in the middle of the mighty Hume Weir. A Saturday morning tram to Spencer Street Station, train to Wodonga, rail motor out to Tallangatta, stay with a local family, take three services on Sunday, return to Otira on Monday and catch up on missed lectures. Each week I approached the weekend with anxiety levels rising. Yet week after week I received valuable lessons on the rural geography, demography and Methodist ecclesiology of Victoria.

In April, Mr. Pederick broke the news to me that my married sister Margaret had taken gravely ill. All the fellows rallied around with comfort and prayer. Margaret deteriorated and Peddo drove me across Melbourne in his little *DKW* auto to Essendon Airport. My brother Ray met me at Launceston Airport and rushed me to join the rest of the family who were gathered around Margaret's bedside at the General Hospital.

She regained consciousness briefly and recognised me. "Bruce?" she whispered. "Bruce... I must be... "

"Yes," said my mother, stroking her forehead, "You are, my darling, and you are very precious to us all." She did not regain consciousness.

We saw Margaret die in the dark hours of the following morning. She left her devastated husband Henry Taylor, seven-year-old daughter Anne and five-year-old Philip. I now knew, firsthand, how much raw grief is like having something tender and deeply treasured violently ripped from one's being.

How could a God of love permit such things to happen to my devout sister? How would Henry manage with his two little children?

But from that time on I have lived the rest of my life with those same dark, unanswerable questions to which no believer or philosopher can give an adequate answer. It is sufficient to learn existentially that God loves us utterly, including when we walk in the valley of the shadow of death.

I saw Marie only briefly during the few days I was home in Launceston. She was busy nursing (night duty) and for most of the time I was occupied with our family, and with the dozens of kindly visitors that came to our house in Alanvale Road to express their condolences. It would be the September vacation before our love for each other could be nourished, face to face. For now, letters must continue to do.

Back in Melbourne I survived a period of depression; grateful to be cared for and absorbed back into the routine of college activities. In the May vacation, generous-hearted Brian Smith took me to his home at McKinnon, to stay with his caring family.

During my time studying at Otira, I countered the inevitable banter about being a *Taswegian* by making sure I topped class in all three terms. I recall composing some rollicking verses for the final graduation/concert evening; doggerel which included a humorous riposte at my kindly, Victorian tormentors.

At the end of the year, instead of being sent for a couple for years to a Home Mission appointment, as was the usual practice for raw recruits like me, the 'powers that be' decided that I should be fast-tracked. With about 25 other young hopefuls, I fronted up to the stringent selection processes for Candidates for the Methodist Ministry. I was much relieved when at the Annual Conference my name appeared among the 15 who were accepted for training.

However, because I had not yet matriculated, legally I could not reside in Queens College, University of Melbourne. The church 'fathers' arranged for me to live for the year (1951) with the Assistant Professor of Theology, Norman Lade, and his dear wife Christine. That was to be a 'one-off' arrangement. It never happened before or after to any other student. From that kindly home, I attended theological lectures at Queens and studied for matric at *Taylors Coaching College*, in Little Collins Street, Melbourne.

I matriculated with honours in all subjects and for the following three years lived in Queens College as a 'log' doing Arts and some theology, homiletics and church governance. In arts I majored in English, philosophy and history, as well as doing one year of basic science and Modern Hebrew. I also spent (misspent?) considerable time on the cricket field, tennis courts and chasing muddy footballs.

For the first year, I shared a study bedroom with a loveable engineering student, a Sikh named Jug Jeet Singh Bulla. An invaluable experience, it left an indelible ecumenical imprint on my soul. The following two years brought me the privilege of rooming with fellow 'log' David Beswick, to whom I could always submit aspects of my gut-instinct, poetic-theology for some systematic critique.

During the first summer vacation I became a student pastor in the Paterson Street Circuit with Rev. Guv Inglis, and in a later year in South Launceston, with Rev. Wilf Manzoney. Visiting patients in hospitals usually sent my anxiety level soaring to about an eight out of ten. Later, for one vacation, I worked as a labourer with the builder Norm Wing, while the final year was spent in the North Melbourne Mission under the eye of the irrepressible Rev. Tom Harvey, where I learnt not to believe the plausible story of every cadger who came looking for a handout.

While I had been living with Prof. Lade, Marie's parents had moved to Camberwell, her dad becoming the *Victorian State Secretary for Overseas Missions*. I would spend some Sundays with her parents, while Marie enjoyed some of her days off with my folk at Alanvale. An odd but helpful arrangement. My mum, dad and big brother Ray, soon came under the spell of MJ's cheerful chatter and accounts of her escapades.

In September 1951, Marie and I proudly announced our engagement. The next year she finished general nursing and came to the Queen Victoria Hospital in Melbourne to study midwifery. After her graduation, she enjoyed some months employed as a qualified midwife in the labour ward. It was wonderful for us to have more time together, but in some ways it made the brief times together, followed by the inevitable partings, even more painful.

While living in Queens College, my keen love for reading and writing poetry posed a brief temptation. Other theologs had their specific temptations; some to switch to medicine, social work, teaching or academia. One part of me would have longed to undertake post-grad studies in English and go on to be a working poet. I sat in the beautiful Queens Chapel and wrestled with this issue. I am not sure when this was resolved, but it was. In the last months at Queens I again said a deep 'yes' to my call and vowed to use my language skills as best I could in the preparation of the legion of sermons that lay ahead of me.

Student days came to an end in 1954. We both were on tenterhooks, waiting to see if I would be given permission by the Methodist Conference to marry. One's first parish appointment often did not have a manse provided. Our immediate happiness hung on that slender thread. I told Professor Calvert Barber in my final interview before leaving Queens College, that I was willing to go anywhere as long as I could be married.

That time, from November 1954 to late February 1955, seemed an interminable wait. Marie had warned me that if we did not get permission, she would go to Brisbane to study for her 'Mothercraft Certificate', rather than endure more of the almost intolerable meeting-and-parting that my calling had imposed on us.

*Launceston General Hospital
@ the elm tress under which
M & B first kissed.*

*Nurse Marie Goldsmith 1950
Launceston General Hospital*

*"Otira" 1950, BP is second
from left, back row.*

*Queens College cricket team
1952 BP front right*

*BP & "Goliath" car, 1955
honeymoon Apollo Bay*

*M & B engagement time
Manse Invermay, Sep 1951*

*Sister Goldsmith
Nurses Home, 1953*

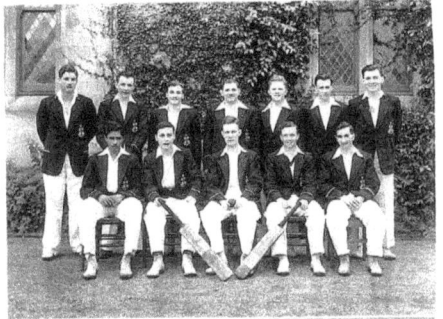

David Beswick – Best Man, Jean Goldsmith – Bridesmaid

South Camberwell Methodist Church,
Saturday 26th March 1955

Mr. and Mrs. Bruce David Prewer

The Bride and Groom with their Attendants

The Bride's parents, George and Jessie Goldsmith

The Groom's parents, Cliff and Florrie Prewer

Bruce David Prewer and Marie Joyce Goldsmith
signing the Register

Rev. Alf Milligan and Rev. George Goldsmith presiding

The Bride and Groom with their parents

The Bride's family, including Jean and Ron Goldsmith

The Groom's family, including Dorothy, Don and
Margaret Ramage (14 months)

Siblings – Marie, Ron and Jean

Mabel and Jack Plant gave the wedding cake

Flowers – from Florrie Prewer's garden, Alanvale
Bridal car – supplied by Mabel and Jack Plant

The happy couple

MY FIRST FULL~TIME MINISTRY

Our fate rested in the (sometimes clumsy) hands of the Stationing Committee. Prof. Calvert Barber reported my willingness to 'go anywhere' to the Stationing Committee and they promptly placed my name against King Island, set in the middle of Bass Strait.

Hallelujah! Our marriage was really going to happen!

We hastily arranged a wedding in the South Camberwell Church, with the rites being shared by George Goldsmith and the Rev. Alf Milligan. The long wait and extended sexual frustration were at last over. We had our honeymoon at 'Greenacres', Apollo Bay, then stayed a week with family friends, Jack and Mabel Plant, on their farm at Daylesford.

A quick pack up of our few possessions followed. We purchased a small car, mainly with Marie's precious savings, and then boarded an old DC3 plane to go for our 'two year island honeymoon'. Bass Strait and the 'roaring forties' became a reality; it proved to be exceedingly windy. There were 107 recorded major shipwrecks on the coast of this one small island.

On a windy morning in April 1955, we arrived and were met by a taciturn Senior Circuit Steward called Ray Heinrich. He delivered us to the small fibro-board parsonage in Currie. We felt very lucky. One predecessor and his wife had to live in the garage for some months while that little house was being built.

Two days later my boss, Rev. John Cousins, arrived from Devonport for my induction in the weatherboard, 'listing-to-port' Currie Church, literally propped up against the incessant wind. The next morning John flew out, but not before giving me his final charge: "Look boy, there are some odd people in this circuit. From time to time they will write letters of complaint to me. Be assured I will read them, but then file them in the waste paper basket and forget them. I have full faith in you. Go for it." Now that is what I call reasonable management!

There were indeed some odd people who wrote letters, including the gloomy Mr. Hienrich. But there were also some wonderful Christians on the island whose choice lives still fill me with gratitude. Folk like the farming Skipworth family north of Grassy, the Bowlings at Surprise Bay, the Trebilcocks at Mt. Stanley, Bishops and Pegarah and some newer arrivals like the Dutch Lewincamps at Yambacoona, and the Cookes at

Yarra Creek. At Currie, we especially enjoyed the friendship of a young June Crack and her fiancé Brian Smith.

Under the Methodist system, I was placed on *probation* for two years. This meant completing more Biblical and theological studies, along with serving the four churches and three 'preaching places'. It might be only a small island, but some Sundays I would travel 160 kilometers on its unsealed roads as I weaved around the places of worship.

My vehicle at this stage was a small, German-made *Goliath;* the post-war, sleek version of the two-stroke DKW that dear old Peddo at Otira had driven. Fortunately, there were no steep hills on the island. Even when driving over Mt. Stanley I only had to change out of overdrive into third gear. On one occasion, with the wind blowing a gale and the road slippery from rain, I suddenly found the Goliath parallel in the scrub – a big gust had, in a split second, pushed me sideways off the road. A bit of body paint would be needed at Yeoman's Garage.

Marie and I settled in well. We were much in love and we had waited so many years. She did some nursing at the local hospital. I revived the youth club, visited assiduously and preached my heart out – asking Christ to stand at my elbow. Marie and I met some wonderful 'soldier settlers' on their newly cleared KI (King Island) parcels of raw farming land; I fished for black-back salmon, played cricket and football with the Currie teams and completed my two years of probationer studies.

There were a number of 'firsts' for this raw young minister. Each 'first' was approached with acute anxiety. My first baptism, first marriage, first funeral; each of these was singularly memorable.

At my first baptism, I chased the father of the baby into the tea-tree scrub to round him up and oblige him to at least stand beside his wife as she took her vows for the upbringing of their little son.

My first marriage was a disaster from the start; the bride's father was drunk and fell over backwards as he delivered her to the side of her soon-to-be husband, to the raucous laughter of his drinking mates in the back seat. The reception was worse; it outdid the famous Munich Beer Festival.

Poignant indeed was the first funeral I had to conduct. A tiny white coffin of a still-born was ferried to the cemetery in the back of an old Chevy 4, with only the undertaker and the grieving father present with me at the graveside. Things did not get easier. My second funeral was a five-year-old child who tragically hanged himself with his shirt on a paling fence while trying to climb over to a neighbour's backyard.

Happier things were happening with a new (Methodist Youth Fellowship) youth group. Each Friday about 20-25 young people gathered with Marie and me in a large room at the back of the church. We had lots of fun and together faced some serious challenges. I wrote a theme song and sent to Melbourne for our own KI MYF badges for each member.

There were many weddings, not just of Methodist people. There was no resident Roman Catholic priest and there were breaks between Anglican ones. There was also no pharmacy on the island. Nearly all weddings were young brides, usually 'with child'. Always the minister was expected to be the MC at the wedding reception. Life was eventful and I was learning from my many mistakes.

Much to our enormous delight, Marie soon became pregnant. After an intense and incapacitating period of morning sickness, we eagerly awaited the arrival of the bub. In all my life, time has not dragged as much as those few months.

Fortunately we were both sea lovers and there was plenty of coast to visit on KI for a picnic. However, as time went by it became too much – there was nowhere else to go while enjoying a few hours off, just the surrounding restless, cold ocean.

Evidently, once KI had been covered with tall eucalyptus forest. But it had all been burnt out by bush fires during early years of settlement. Now only tea-tree scrub remained. I decided I did not have an affinity for the ubiquitous tea-tree. On one occasion we drove out to Pegarah, just to sit by the side of the road under a couple of tall gum tress that had survived. Because we were as poor as the proverbial church mice, we could not afford the plane fare to get off for any regular visits to our respective families in Victoria and Tasmania.

We were worried that the parsonage did not have a fridge. With a baby arriving soon, we were concerned about the safety of kept food, for both mother and infant. (We could not afford one. Often my stipend was late, and even when we finally completed our term on the island, some arrears in traveling expenses were never paid.)

A letter arrived from a dear lady in Horsham. She said that Deaconess Hilda Fisher, of the Home Missions Department, had been speaking at her church and had mentioned that the young minister's wife on KI did not have a fridge. She enclosed a cheque to cover the cost of a new fridge. We wrote back our effusive thanks and soon had a wonderful, shiny new fridge installed in our small lounge – the kitchen was too small and there was only an external shed for a laundry.

That laundry made 'washing day' hard work. I lit and stoked the fire under a large copper. Marie hand-washed, using a multi-ribbed 'washing board', then boiled the clothes, stirring frequently with and old broom handle. Finally she rinsed it all in the concrete 'washing-trough', dipped all the whites through a 'blue-bag' bath, put all items through a hand-turned wringer and finally hung the washing on a long single clothes line. At least the drying was easy – there was always a wind.

The 19ᵗʰ of January was to be a high point of our lives. After an extensive labour (with no husband permitted to be present to give his support) Marie brought forth our first bundle of delight, David Andrew. Over 50 years on, I clearly remember that morning. Her mum, Jess Goldsmith, had flown over a few days before. As I arrived home from shopping at about 10am, she came out into the yard to me with the news. I almost dropped our just-repaired, precious wireless that belonged to Marie. Mouth widely agape, I stood there in the wind and sunshine amazed at the miracle of being a dad.

As soon as we were allowed by the regimented hospital routine, we visited Marie and welcomed little David Andrew into our arms. Marie Joyce was a wonderful young mother, caring for her newborn with wonder shining in her eyes. So besotted was I that for days (no, for weeks) I could hardly concentrate on my work. Little David Andrew was the rapture of our lives. I was a doting, and let it be said, much sleep-deprived dad. Not surprisingly, our new little King Islander was a windy baby and suffered from colic.

Six weeks later we flew to Melbourne for the annual Methodist Conference. At Camberwell, on a glorious autumn day, George Goldsmith baptised David. At some evening sessions of Conference we joyfully met up with our many friends and colleagues. I got the ear of Deaconess Hilda Fisher and thanked her for her good word while speaking at Horsham. She looked puzzled and insisted she never knew a thing about our situation on KI, in fact had no idea there had been a need for a fridge. Strange? Such is the prodigal grace and ingenuity of God.

We returned to our island home, feeling more acutely a sense of isolation out there in the middle of Bass Strait, with my parents in Tasmania and Marie's in Victoria.

My boss, the Rev. John Cousins, came for a supervisor's visit in late March. We reviewed many aspects of my ministry on King Island. John was on a 'high' following a very successful professional stewardship campaign that his own congregation at Devonport had recently completed. I pumped him for details of the campaign. I took notes. After talking it through with Marie, I decided we would attempt to direct a campaign of our own using similar methodology.

We were able to sell the idea to a handful of key laypeople. Directing our own campaign was very hard work, but the result was encouraging. What happened in the process was an eye-opener. Many who were strongly challenged about the use of money experienced a spiritual renewal. The planned-giving of the King Island Methodists increased offerings fivefold. However, our churches were still not self-supporting and we had to rely on grants and other outside assistance.

For months Marie had not been able to successfully bake anything in the old, burnt out, wood-fueled oven. The Rev. Ern Baker paid a pastoral visit to us, saw the situation and went back to a women's group in Launceston with a request. Before long, a glorious new slow-combustion stove, with a hot water facility, was installed. A tank was erected, high on a stand, at the rear of the laundry to provide water pressure. Each morning and evening I exercised the hand pump for 15 minutes to keep that tank full.

Baths whenever we wanted them at the turn of a tap! No more 'chip heater' in the bathroom with its sawdust and ashes! No more boiling every cuppa on the small, pump-up primus stove. We now had a fridge and hot water. Paradise!

The following year, in early February 1957, Marie's mum and dad and her teenage brother Ron, arrived for a visit. We showed them all the sights of the island, from the mining township of Grassy by the East Coast, to the lighthouse at Point Wickham in the North, to the wild shores around Currie on the West Coast. No shortage of seascapes for them to view!

Ron and I went fishing at Sea Elephant Inlet. Loving the isolation, he stripped bare and got badly sunburnt where he had never been burnt before! Egged on by Ron, "have a zing at it, have a zing at it", I took a rifle, shot at a duck and guiltily bagged it out of season. We knew little about native ducks. Trying to cook it we soon discovered it was a highly aromatic musk duck, quite inedible. Served us right, eh?

In late February, the six of us set our sights on Melbourne. The Annual Conference was held in February/March and I was to be ordained. We gathered apprehensively with other passengers in the tiny 8 x 6 metre terminal building while the pilot and his offsider calculated the weight of passengers and luggage and whether he would be able to coax the DC3 up off the runway. After a few passengers agreed to leave some excess baggage behind for a later flight, we all boarded with some apprehension. We made it. Just. The plane's wheels cleared the fence and the tea-tree scrub with what appeared to be about three metres to spare.

On the 7th March 1957, I was accepted 'into full connexion' and ordained, along with 14 others, in front of a packed Wesley Church in Lonsdale Street. The same week it became official that we were to be stationed at Wynyard, on the NW coast of Tasmania, for the next few years.

Good, pious religion should lead me to report that the ordination service was an exhilarating, spiritual event. Truth forbids me to so avow. Suffering from an extremely heavy cold, every canal in my head seemed inflamed. I was ordained in a personal mental fog. Divinely inspired the event certainly was, that I believe with all my mind and heart. That certainty has stayed with me all the following 66 busy years. But exhilarating for me it was not, that night in Wesley Church.

The Methodist Church of Australasia

Victoria and Tasmania Conference

Order of the

Ordination Service

Back Row: W. L. Goldsworthy, J. R. Lawton, J. K. Smith, D. L. Rowe, B.Com.;
A. W. Collins, E. B. Cousins, D. H. Hunt, W. L. Swaby, B.A.
Front Row: O. P. Marett, A. B. Body, B.A.; M. S. Box, B.A.; M. E. Stansall, B.A.;
B. D. Prewer, B.A.; R. G. Williams, B.A.; J. E. Richards.

WESLEY CHURCH

Thursday Evening, 7th March, 1957

at 7.30 o'clock

Family snaps showing David, Martin and Christine

WONDERFUL WYNYARD

April 1957 to December 1961

With agile David trotting down the plane gangway ahead of us, we arrived at Wynyard to be met by the most hospitable Senior Circuit Steward, Russ York, and his lovely wife Joy. Their lovely smiles were a contrast to that phlegmatic welcome we received two years earlier to our first appointment on King Island.

They delivered us and our baggage to the Methodist parsonage at 44 Hogg Street, showed us the layout and then whisked us up to Yolla to their farm house for a superb roast lamb and vegs luncheon. Then back to our new abode in Hogg Street and the inevitable unpacking of many tea chests of possessions.

A phone call came from my brother-in-law Don Ramage. He had readily agreed to collect our Goliath motor car at the Devonport wharf when the island trading ship, the *Willwatch,* berthed. He said there was both bad news and good news. The bad news was that the small ship had been caught in a storm and a Holden Ute had gone overboard to the bottom of Bass Straight. The good news was that although our Goliath was damaged, it was drivable. Don had watched the Willwatch come up the Mersey River, my vehicle hanging over the side, held only by its front wheels. The wharfies then manually, and most gingerly, lifted it on to the wharf.

Poor Goliath! I collected it, gave it to a bodyworks in Wynyard and received it back with a new paint job. But from that time on there was a succession of engine troubles. My mechanic believed that the chassis had been distorted on its epic voyage and this had placed too much pressure on some mechanical parts.

But things were to become far worse for the Willwatch. During that same year she disappeared without a trace in Bass Straight. Among the crew was a lad called Neville Chitts who had been a member of our KI youth group.

Wynyard was a big challenge for a young minister. Three or four services each Sunday and five once a month, and six schools to be visited each week for Religious Instruction. There were substantial congregations at Wynyard and Yolla and smaller though loyal ones at Mt. Hicks, Sisters Creek, Flowerdale and Moorleah. Yolla held Christian Endeavour for the young folk, while a youth group flourished at Wynyard. I loved the work of ministry, threw myself 100% into everything, but was in danger of what is now called 'burn out'.

Looking back, I wonder whether I also risked 'burn out' in some of our lay leaders?

I became more aware that my anxiety was never going away. Before any up-front-happening, the worry levels would rise dramatically. Simple duties, like entering a school class room, walking up into the pulpit, lobbying local councillors, meeting visiting church dignitaries, going into hospitals and nursing homes – all of these used up more precious adrenalin than was good for me. I tried to cope with this by increasing my prayer life – rising at 6am or taking half a day off to spend alone out in the bush.

At that time I saw anxiety as a lack of faith. I was not always easy to live with. When I read in a published prayer by 'The Man Called Peter' (Rev. Peter Marshall of the USA) of stomach ulcers being a 'badge of our faithlessness', I further blamed myself for my innate timidity.

A big blessing of the Wynyard Circuit was the fine lay leadership that surrounded me in my youthful enthusiasm. I never felt alone in my tasks. It may be unfair to only name certain people but I will mention one. Viv Byard, father of the inimitable Rev. Trevor Byard, who was then in his 60s, became my prayer partner and consultant. Viv had made his share of mistakes (some of them big ones) in his Christian journey. He was the wiser for it. I could always pour out my heart to him. He could lovingly affirm or confront me, and enable me to clarify my thinking. Sadly, when I was a couple of years into this term of ministry, I was thrown into grief when dear Viv suddenly died from heart failure.

My other mainstay was Russ York. What a choice Christian soul he was! Like all genuinely good people, he never knew it and would be embarrassed to read it in this document.

Among other duties, as the Senior Circuit Steward, Russ had to keep the financial books. At that task he was almost as inept as I was. Once every three months we met for a day at the parsonage to prepare the Financial Statement for the Circuit Quarterly Meeting. It was like raspberry seeds under a denture – for both of us. But we managed. And the 'fellowship in suffering' was memorable. What a heavenly relief it was when bank a manager and fine Christian, Bob Nichol – with his lovely wife Mary and their lively twin daughters – arrived in town and lifted that load off our shoulders.

David was to have a sibling. Marie was happily pregnant. On 6th October 1957, Martin George (in honour of the Protestant Reformer and also of his grandfather, George Goldsmith) was born at the Wynyard Hospital. Because of some obtuse hospital regulation, other children were not allowed in to see the mother of the new baby. A nurse held Martin up to a window for David to look from the outside while he sat on my shoulders. His comment was: "How did they get it out Daddy?"

Grandma Prewer came down by train from Launceston to help care for David and me. To her chagrin, while under her care, David rushed behind a heavy swing and was concussed.

He was admitted to hospital. For some crazy reason, his Mummy was not allowed to visit him from the maternity ward and he needed her very much. I had to substitute, but our darling little boy was not a happy chappy.

I had to leave David's bedside to attend to some church matters. On returning, I found him strapped up in a straightjacket! It seems they had caught him trying to leave hospital to find his way home. I was furious that they had done this to a small child. I unbuckled him, gathered him up from the bed, and ignoring the fierce cries of the ward Sister "You cannot do that!", I stormed out of the hospital and took David home to his grandmother's warm arms.

That Sister never did get over my flouting of her authority. Nor did I get over my distaste for the cruel thing she had done to my son. Thereafter, whenever I visited other patients, some frost would settle within that particular ward.

Grandma, David and I were relieved when Marie and Martin were able to come home. A week later, Grandma Prewer went back to Launceston. We were now a close-knit family of four. Martin was a gorgeous little chap, much less restless than his brother, and before long blessed with the most heart-melting smile. Marie and I now had two sons to be besotted with.

I made one (at least) bad mistake as a husband and father during those early years. I was too conscientious about church responsibilities, to the detriment of my wife and children. Hectic days were followed by busy evenings, with much counselling or church meetings. I gravely repent my lopsided life and am so grateful that neither Marie nor my children ever hated me for it. Marie is indeed an exceptional woman. Looking back, I am so blessed that she did not up and leave that work-obsessed young minister who attempted to be 'all things to all people', except to those in his own family.

Lest anyone assume I was never there for them, let me at least state this: I tried to be available late afternoon to spend some time with the kids. By the age of four years, David could kick a football better than I could. Martin, even as a toddler, loved being carried around the back garden on Daddy's shoulders, or later on, with a cheeky grin, bobbing off by himself looking for ripe strawberries, or even for gooseberries among the prickles. After dinner each evening, I would squeeze in time to help put them to bed and share their night prayers.

Nevertheless I lament those days off I never did take. A Monday off with my darling MJ was rare. No wonder our annual holidays were such a big event. Usually vacation was taken at my parents' cottage at Bridport – a seaside haven forever etched in the mind of my family. But even from there, one time I was called back to Wynyard for two days in order to attend to the funeral of a lad from the Methodist youth club who had drowned while fishing in the Inglis River. The allotted three weeks vacation was not enough!

It was not just the Wynyard Circuit that took my time and energy. I was expected to lead at least one North West District youth camp each year and drive with others along to the Launceston meetings of the Tasmanian Assembly Executive Committee. I was also inveigled into planning and compering the bi-monthly 'Call to Youth' gatherings for the region. These were attended by between 500-800 young people and were held on Saturday nights in centres from Devonport to Wynyard. It would often be well after midnight and Sunday morning, before I returned home to snatch a few hours of sleep before tackling another round of Sunday worship.

No wonder I developed severe 'nervous dyspepsia' and was ordered by my GP to take a fortnight off. We flew to Melbourne and, goaded by George and Jess Goldsmith, sought treatment from the remarkable Rev. Arthur Lelean at Ballarat. To my surprise it worked.

Yet I did not fully accept, even after that protracted time recovering from glandular fever, that there was an obsessive kink in my psyche. I always wanted to do more and more for the kingdom of God, could not seem to reign myself in. This was a grievous fault, not a virtue! I still wrestle with elements of that obsessive kink.

For relaxation, during the summers I played cricket with the Wynyard A grade team. The press featured me alongside fellow cricketer Oz Marrett of Smithton and Warren Clarnette (tennis) of East Devonport, as 'the three sporting parsons'. That did not hurt my public profile in Wynyard either.

Although congregations were flourishing numerically, our circuit finances were static. After one dismal failure at running our own stewardship campaign, we managed to get majority support for a program run by the *Methodist Department of Stewardship Promotion.* We were assigned the good-humoured, irrepressible Brian Jones as Director. That proved to be a mighty step forwards, both spiritually and financially. Inevitably there were a few folk, until then busy workers within the church, who could not hack the challenge of stewardship and to my grief, they dropped out.

Brain Jones was a smoker. Young Martin became fascinated and began to souvenir Brian's cigarette butts. He would put up a struggle whenever we tried to dispossess him of these treasures. After Brian had left Wynyard, Martin took to picking up butts from footpaths. Marie and I were now worried about the heath implications. One sunny morning in my study, I produced a new fag, lit it and handed to him, "There my boy, enjoy. Suck in big." He eagerly did just that. Gasping for fresh air, his face first turned a vivid red and then a pallid green. So ended little Martin's obsession with cigarette butts.

During a bout of glandular fever, while I was laid up for a couple of weeks, I read a book by noted British Anglican evangelist Canon Bryan Green. His advice inspired me to attempt a more high profile outreach. Utilising the churches' column of the local north-west newspaper *The Advertiser,* leaflet dropping homes listed as Methodist and erecting large billboards around the township, we organised and advertised a month's special evening services.

The first Sunday over 350 people crowded into the Wynyard Church. The choirmaster wryly complained that he had to drive his car back home to find parking. By the fourth week, attendance had slipped back to about 270. It was deemed a remarkable first attempt, and resulted in new commitments to Christ and a long-term increase in church attendances.

Writing poetry, even hasty scrawlings, was a rare event. Most of my creativity seemed to be spent on worship, sermons and writing a couple of study booklets (run off on the ubiquitous 'Gestetner' and hand stapled!) for youth and children's camps.

The following year, on the 13th February 1960, our daughter Christine Lyn was born after a mercifully brief labour for Marie. I was over the moon to have a daughter as well as our two sons. When the phone rang with the news, I did somersaults up the long central passage of the parsonage. Marie could not contain her happiness. She had a *daughter!* She really was a 'blooming' mother. Once again, dearest Grandma Prewer travelled by train to help care for our two boys while Marie and Chris were in hospital. They loved her cuddles and cooking – lots of scones, biscuits and decorated cup-cakes.

I now felt my cup was full and overflowing. God had been so good to me, with the gift of Marie Joyce and three lovely children.

Children on an old train, City Park, Launceston, 1959
David and Martin - centre

Boat Harbour, December 1959

David in the backyard at Wynyard
December 1959

Christmas Day 1959

David and Martin at Wynyard Parsonage
December 1959

In front of Wynyard State School
December 1959

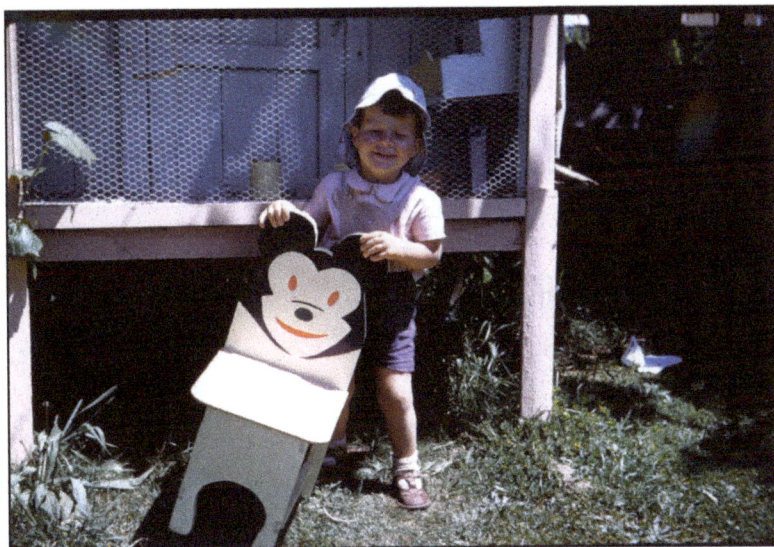

Martin at Wynyard
December 1959

Wynyard Parsonage
1959

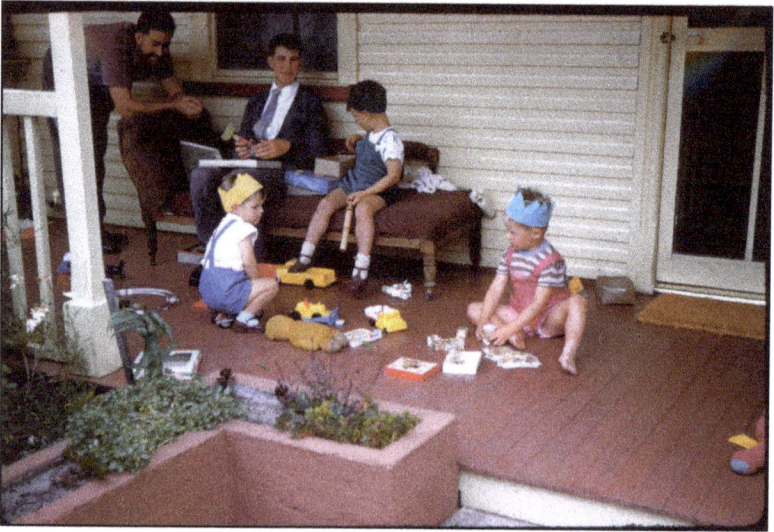

Ray, Martin, Phillip, David and Andrew
Christmas Day 1959

Wynyard Sunday School Picnic
December 1959

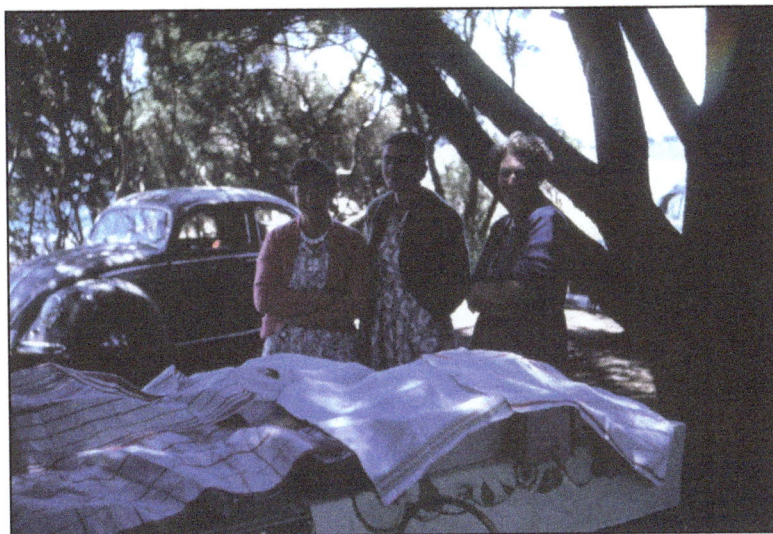

Wynyard Sunday School Picnic
December 1959

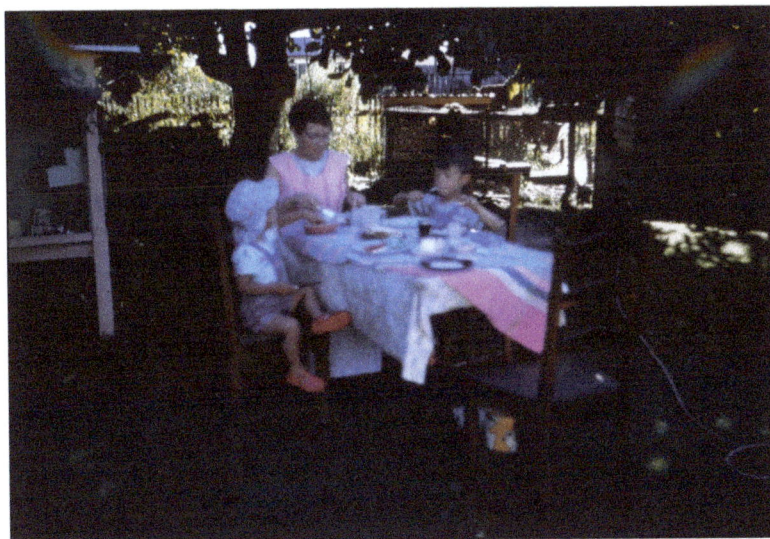

Martin, Marie and David
Backyard at Wynyard, January 1960

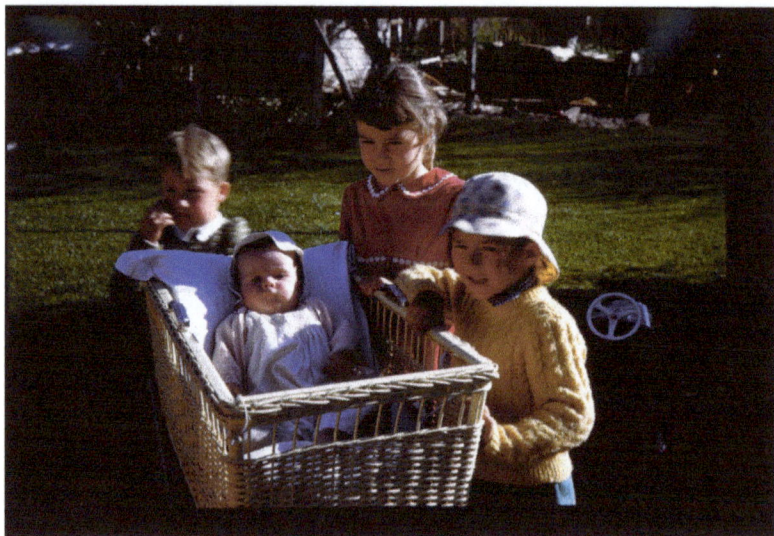

Andrew, Christine, Kim and David
Wynyard

Alanvale
January 1960

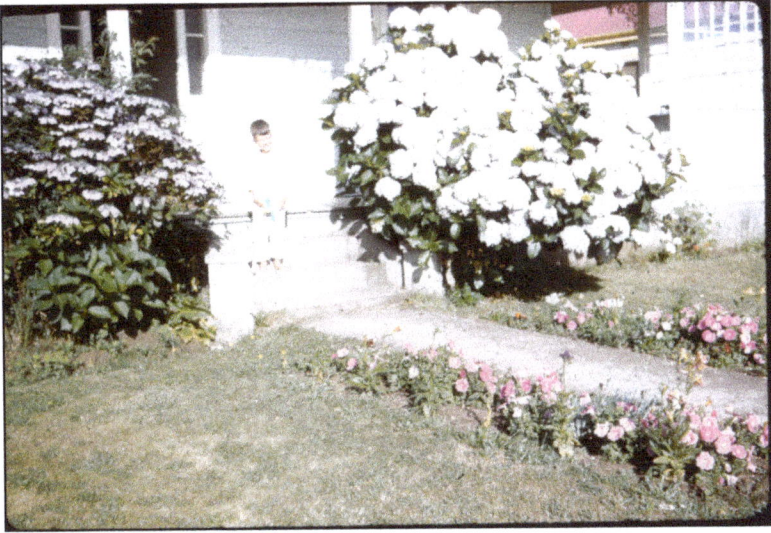

David on the front porch at Wynyard
January 1960

David at Launceston Conservatory
January 1960

Western Tiers
January 1960

Pop (Cliff), Marie and David at the junction
of the Mersey and Fisher Rivers, Western Tiers
January 1960

Near Wynyard
1960

Above and below
David's 4th birthday, Alanvale
January 1960

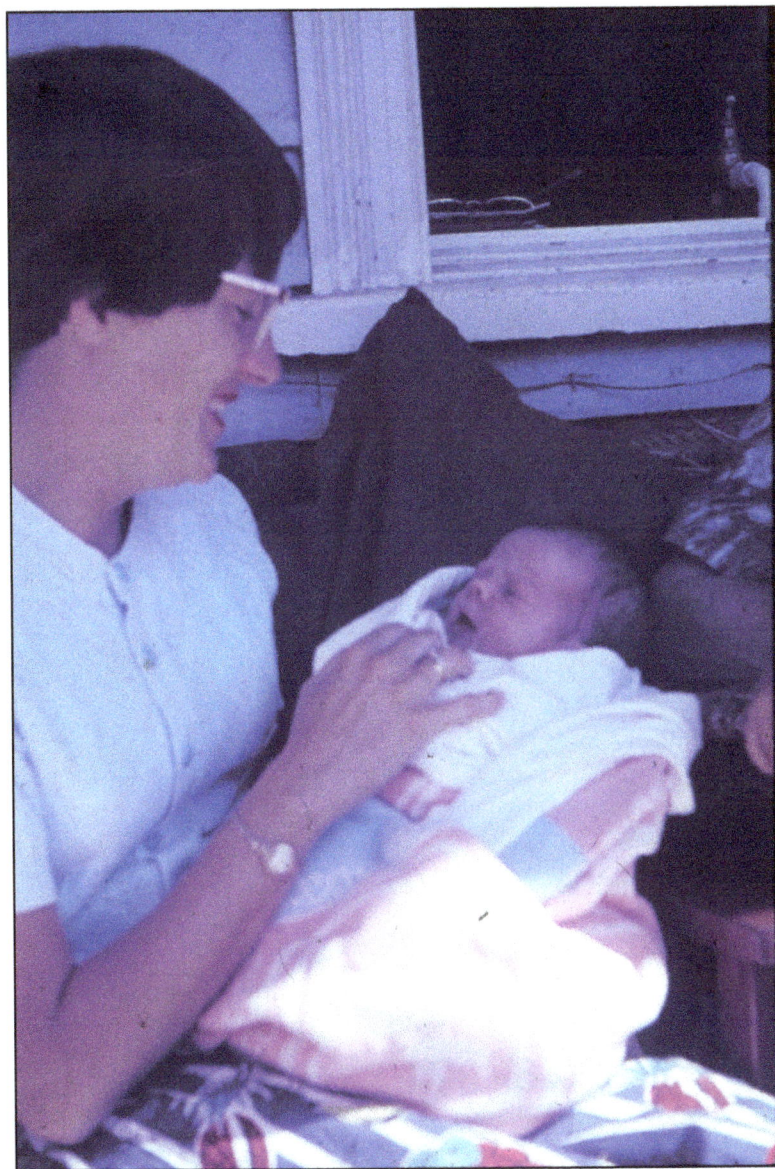

Marie with Christine, two weeks old
28th February 1960

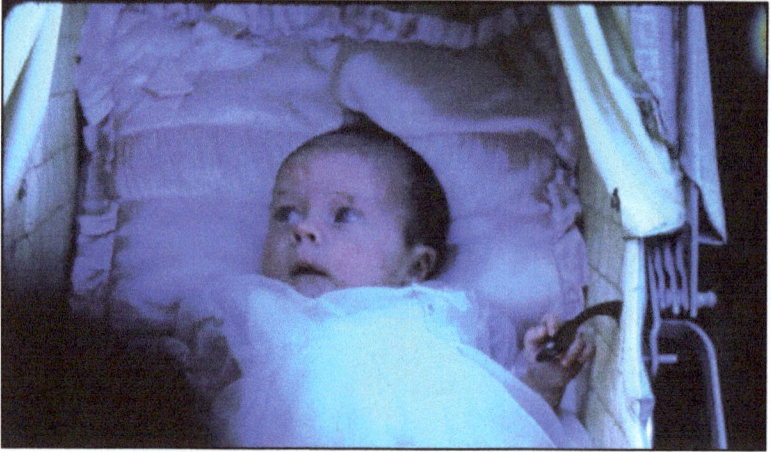

Christine at five weeks
March 1960

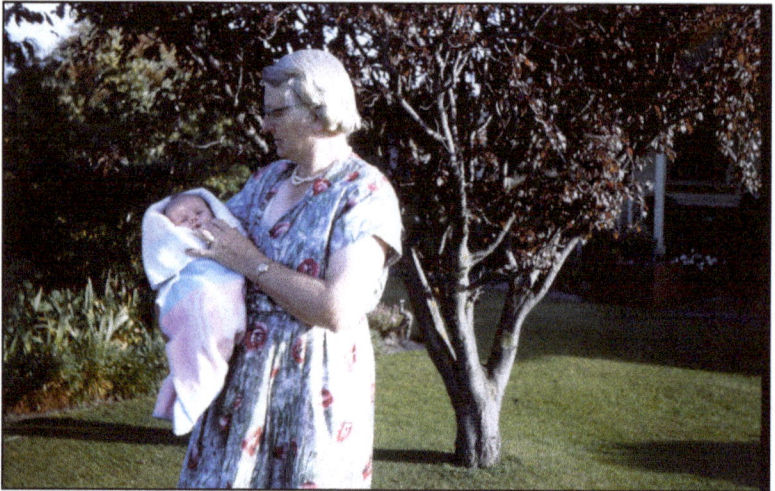

Grandma (Jessie) with Christine at Alanvale
30th March 1960

Blackberrying
March 1960

The North West Coast countryside
March 1960

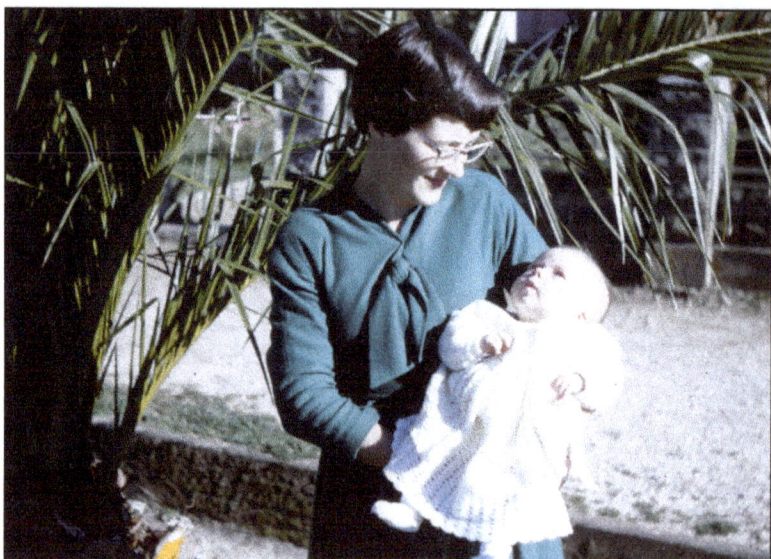

Christine's baptism
22nd May 1960

Heazlewood, Spry, Imms and Prewer families at a picnic
May 1960

David at Wynyard
1960

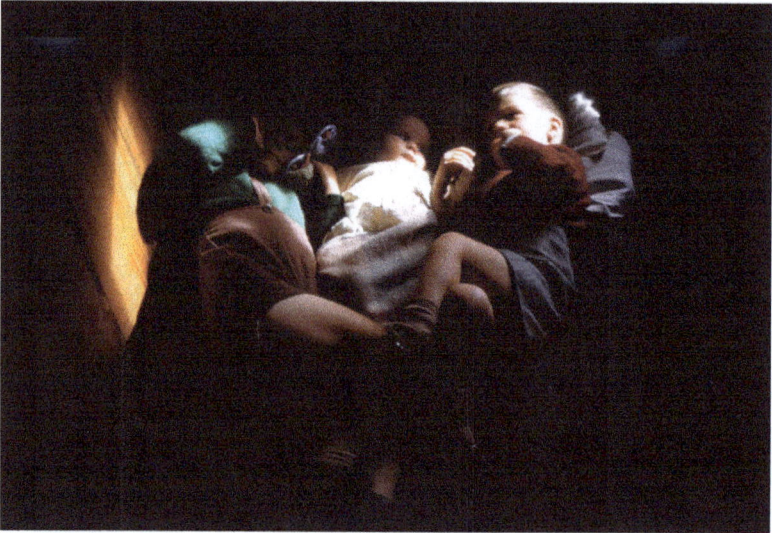

David, Christine and Martin, Bridport
September 1960

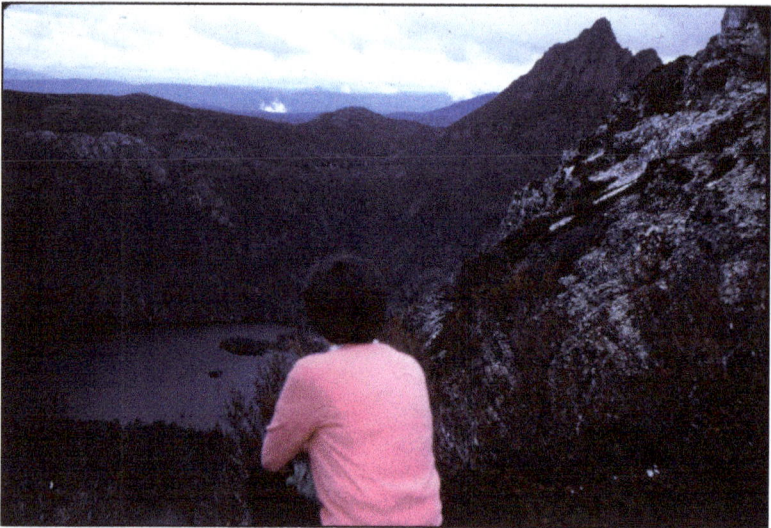

Marie at Cradle Mountain
October 1960

Martin, Marie and David at Fern Glade, Burnie
November 1960

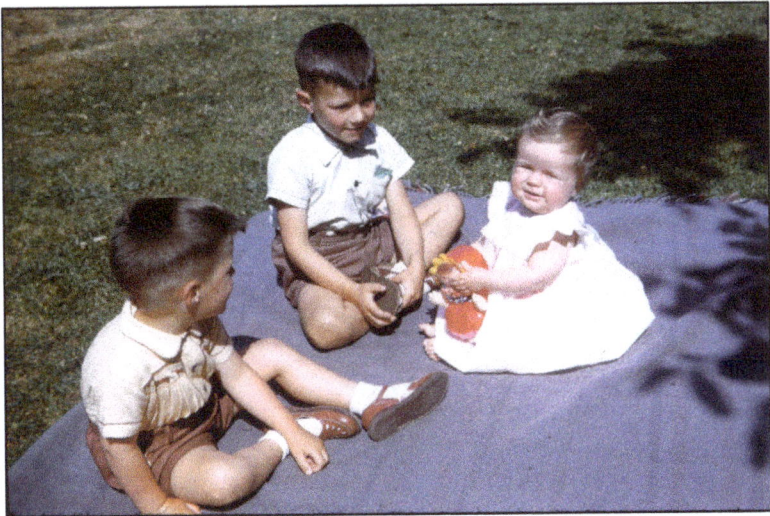

David, Martin and Christine
Christmas Day 1960

Pop Songs At Service To Boost Religion

RHYTHM in CHURCH!

His New Idea

A YOUNG Methodist minister at Wynyard is using pop songs and rock 'n' roll to bring religion closer to the people.

He is 29-year-old Reverend Bruce D. Prewer, who has been minister-in-charge of the Wynyard Methodist Circuit for more than three years.

This month Mr. Prewer is replacing the usual Sunday night services with a new and informal type of Christian teaching.

While his church is being renovated, the church hall is being thrown open each Sunday night to people of all denominations.

Informal Dress

The informal dress-as-you-please evenings start with a talk of about 20 minutes by Mr. Prewer on such challenging questions as: Is There a God? Was Jesus a Fake? and Has Christianity Had It?

After the talk, a layman from the audience is asked to chair the meeting and people are encouraged to disagree or argue on the beliefs put forward.

Afterwards the audience sings pop songs and hit-paraders.

REV. BRUCE PREWER

That winter, while the church building was being renovated, we launched 'Worship with a Difference' each Sunday evening in the church hall. I think it might have been among the first informal worship events in Australia. We employed 'pop' gospel music, lots of singing, a brief sermon, and dared to have a segment of talk back, when members of the congregations could put the minister under pressure with some tough questioning. They did. It was a huge success.

I was challenged by one local sceptic to come out from the safety of the brick church walls and preach on the street. I did so on successive Friday evenings by answering questions on a street corner (backed by a banner), not by literally haranguing the late night shoppers.

This Wynyard happening made it into a national 'scandal rag' of that era which went under the banner of 'The Truth'. My photo was featured alongside a voluptuous Italian film star, Gina Lollolbrigida. One uncle disowned me when he heard of this. That rejection did not cost me too much sleep. The publicity insured the remainder of these informal services had packed congregations. A number of people, including Tasmania's premier football umpire, gave their lives to Christ as a result.

During this stage of my development I became dissatisfied with the extempore prayers which were expected to flow freely from a Methodist minister's mouth. By tape-recording my church services, it became obvious that the same pet phrases and images were heavily overworked. Far from being 'free prayer', it was nearly as repetitive as the *Book of Common Prayer*, but not as beautifully composed. There needed to be more variety. I attempted to improve my vocabulary and imagery by extensively using the prayers of others in my personal devotions, reading them aloud and savouring them, saturating myself with their smooth vocabulary before I went to bed on Saturday nights. This helped a little, yet as my tape recorder revealed, it was not enough. I started to compose some of my own, employing more contemporary folk language.

In late spring, I was backing out of the Wynyard parsonage driveway when I felt a bump and heard a scream. Christine had pushed through the side gate and crawled into the path of the car. My world turned black in one moment. Leaping out of the car I found her crying, but not looking seriously injured. There were rubber tyre marks down her forehead and across her legs. We rushed her to our GP who examined her thoroughly and pronounced her not injured. "Their baby bones are remarkably pliable" he assured us. That night we went to bed as the most grateful parents in whole world.

A month later, I had to conduct a funeral at Yolla for a little boy who had not been so fortunate. A tractor backed over him and killed him. Those poor parents! Such abysmal, intolerable grief! Their nightmare went on and on. Mine slowly faded and was almost gone a few years later.

That year, 1961, the long-standing February/March date for the Methodist Conference was permanently altered. It was to be held thereafter in late September/October. I was moved on from Wynyard by the Stationing Committee and sent to Glenorchy Church, in the large Newtown Circuit. Ironically, I had begged my Chairman of District, the Rev. N Kemp "If I have to move somewhere in Tasmania, let it be anywhere except Glenorchy." I did this because of ructions over finance that had been going on during the two previous years in the Glenorchy congregation of the large, three-minister Newtown Circuit. But the rugged old Chairman, the Rev. Norman Kempo, wanted me there. So that was that. Maybe God also wanted it.

That Christmas we left wonderful Wynyard. After an emotional farewell, we drove to Alanvale, and later to Bridport, for a three week holiday before reporting for duty at Glenorchy.

Lorraine Crescent, Rosetta
1962

A ROOM WITH A VIEW

At Rosetta, we turned off the main highway into Lorraine Crescent. Number One was our destination. We spotted it and gawked!

No parsonage had ever looked like this one. It was modern light cream brick, three levels high – if one included the spacious garage on ground level. We were welcomed at the door by smiling faces of some of our new parishioners who had a light luncheon on the table for us. They handed us the keys, wished us a happy time living here and then mercifully left us to absorb our new home.

The kids explored while Marie and I pinched ourselves. The furnishings were basic but the place was spacious. The top floor held the living quarters: a long kitchen, a massive family room with windows and balcony, a lounge/dining room and a comfortable study looking north.

The main front entrance was via a landing half way between the top floor and the lower floor, where we found five bedrooms, a bathroom, toilet and an under-the-stairs storage room.

The most spectacular feature was the outlook. Talk about a room with a view! This was the grandmother of all views. From the kitchen we looked out to Mt. Wellington and the foothills. The family room had glass on three sides featuring the Derwent River from Cadbury's Point to the end of Elwick Bay, its jutting promontory opposite historic Risdon, and beyond that to a mauve-ish Mt. Rumney.

For people like Marie and me, whose moods are influenced by our setting, this was indeed a healing vista. We never grew tired of enjoying it.

David soon found friends in the small crescent and at the nearby Rosetta State School. Four-year-old Martin was the slowest to settle in. Maybe we had not prepared him enough for the permanent uprooting from his Wynyard home – he loathed this new dwelling. For a while his kinder paintings were all in heavy, unrelieved black. On the other hand, Christine adjusted readily, becoming an unofficial mascot for older girls in the crescent.

Although soon engulfed in the work of the church, I was more circumspect than I had been at Wynyard. I had learned some things from that experience. The major one, and the hardest lesson, was that no matter how much you devote yourself to the people, some parishioners will always be discontented and critical. Therefore, book in some days off for your family. The second lesson was, don't evangelise without making sure there are sound nurture groups in which new members can be cared for and 'grown up in the faith'.

After my induction, I announced that for the first month, I would only attend the basic church meetings, such as the Quarterly and Leaders' Meetings and that of the Property Trustees. My first priority would be calling briefly on every family.

I memorised names before I rang each doorbell. Over five weeks I made snap visits to every family, explaining that it would be a brief visit unless they had immediate issues to discuss with me. I also explained that things inevitably became busier the longer a minister was in a pastorate. If they wished me ever to call to their home again they should not hesitate in asking me. (Of course, to the frail elderly and sick I said I would soon visit them again.)

Most took up the offer of my saying a prayer for their family (each by name) and for their home. By the end of a month, I actually knew the name and face of each adult and child. I believe that the early round of pastoral visiting, wearying though it was, laid a solid groundwork for some of the awkward challenges that lay ahead for both people and pastor.

There were only three congregations for me to look after. That was a luxury following the larger Wynyard experience. Glenorchy Church, which featured a delightful junior choir in the morning and a senior choir in the evening, had the largest congregation by far. Key laypeople like the Eatons, Coopers, Vautins, Betts, Stansalls, and newer members such as Ron Adams and Connie Egan, provided a solid backbone to the congregation. There was a flourishing Sunday School with lots of children, conducted by enthusiastic teachers in some excellent class rooms and a main hall.

Springfield provided a functional set of buildings set in what had been a new, although not large, housing area. The main driving force was the indefatigable Madeleine Ransley and her quiet, reliable (and sometimes long-suffering) husband Ken. The small worship centre was always well filled each Sunday and the Sunday School thrived.

Collinsvale is a picturesque valley tucked between foothills and mountains. There was a small church building with a sparse congregation which met once a fortnight. Once a week I conducted RI in a small school of about 110 pupils, some of whom had never been out of the confines of the valley. When it snowed, making pastoral visits to Collinsvale became a novelty for me.

The attendance during winter at the traditional 7pm service was sparse. It had been held at that time without fail ever since the church was established over 100 years before. The Leaders' Meeting agreed to a proposal that we experiment with a 4.30pm service, advertising it as 'Worship at Dusk'. This proved most successful. These days such an innovation would hardly raise a yawn but at that time it was seen as a radical move. The local paper even featured the young parson's 'daring-do' on a front page.

Unfortunately, there had been that history of Glenorchy Church fighting the rest of the Newtown Circuit about their allocation to circuit and wider church finances. With the goodwill of most of the congregation, I pushed for a separation of the pastorate from the circuit. I saw this as the best way to end the previous bickering. It happened with relative speed and smoothness.

A harder ask was to encourage them to engage the Methodist Department of Stewardship for a confronting, systematic giving program. This did not go down well in some quarters; some of the goodwill in my pastoral bank was evidently exhausted. One comment was "If the Minister can afford to give a tenth of his stipend, then obviously we must be paying him too much." Nevertheless, the majority backed the program and it was for many people a time of deep spiritual renewal.

Over a two-year period, I managed to gain an Honours Bachelor of Divinity, working solo with no access to a library. Marie and the kids were subjected to my muttering Hebrew and Greek while I walked around the house, or as I listened to a tape recording of me reading passages from the Old Testament in Hebrew, as I did the dishes or tended my veggie garden. Looking back, I wonder how my wonderful Marie Joyce put up with it. My God, what a wife she has been!

On the positive side, I still tried to spend definite, set times with David, Martin and Christine before dinner each evening. As a family we managed to tackle some bush walking and mountain climbing.

Easter was always a special time. Grandma and Grandad Prewer and Uncle Ray arrived for a visit, laden not only with Easter eggs, but also with many kinds of edible goodies. We managed to keep two days free at Easter to share special picnics with them in unique settings like the Russell Falls, Bruny Island or Hastings Caves.

About this time I tried to stopped beating myself up about my anxiety and became more analytical. I devised a system where each day I could rate on a graph my mood levels. I found that there appeared to be a 37-day cycle. I was not manic, but there was a slight tendency that way. The graph showed that I slowly went down from a reasonable level of self-confidence to deeper anxiety and timidity over the period. Then in a couple days, I would rise back up. I began to try meditation as distinct from prayer.

I also faced the fact that all authority figures still made me fearful. Senior minsters like Norman Kemp made me tongue-tied. To be pulled over by a policeman left me shaking. Meeting with senior political figures, such as our State Governor, left me reduced to a jelly. Maybe that event in my childhood, when the police traumatised me at school, was to blame?

To my dismay, the Tasmanian Executive co-opted me as the spokesman for the church on social justice issues. I felt out of my depth, but took many deep breaths and gave it my best shot. Press releases on social/political issues always took an inordinate time to compose and courage to deliver. I hated being interviewed on TV. In practical ways I tried to utilise the better times for creative work and person-to-person ministry, and the anxious times for routine jobs in my study.

For some weeks I had to represent the Methodist Church in Tasmania at a Royal Commission into the 'Sunday Observance Act', under the eagle eye of that formidable QC, P.D. Phillips of Melbourne. Basically I submitted (to the surprise of some) that the churches should expect no favours, but argued strongly for some limitation on increased sporting and commercial activity for the wellbeing of all, lest Sunday, as a time when all family members could enjoy time together, should be lost because of increased roster and shift work. The Commissioner agreed. Sadly, the subsequent loss of that one day a week, when a whole family could be free of work responsibilities, has come to pass in the many years since. We are a poorer nation for it.

Bruce Rollins, now working in the Department of Christian Education, asked me to write a study book for the upcoming Methodist Summer Schools. The result, published with the title *The Making of a Servant,* was enthusiastically received. This did my self-image no harm. However, not this success or any other could reach and annul the roots of my self-crippling anxiety.

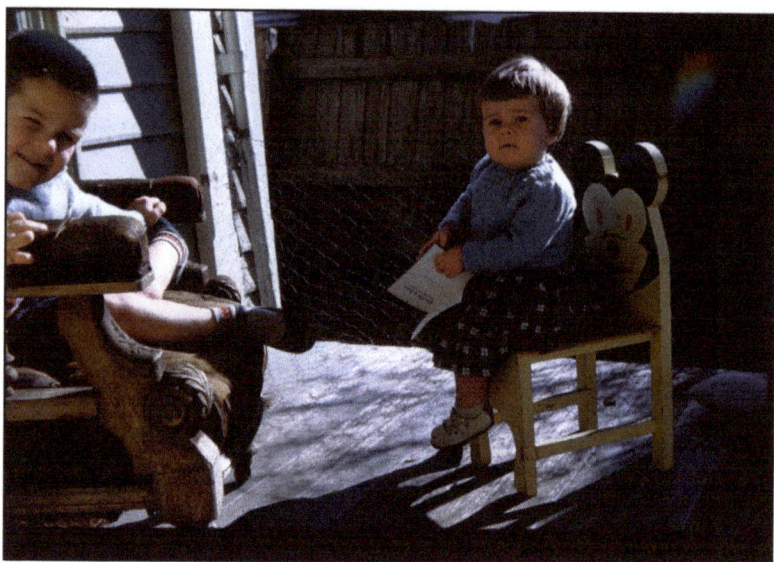

Side porch Wynyard after church
1961

Binalong Bay, St. Helens
January 1961

Coles Bay
January 1961

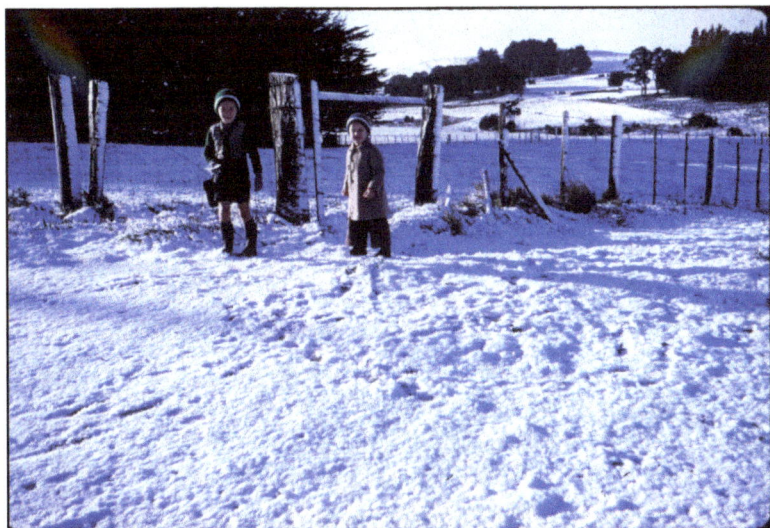

It's cold, but fun!
June 1961

Martin's 4th birthday
1961

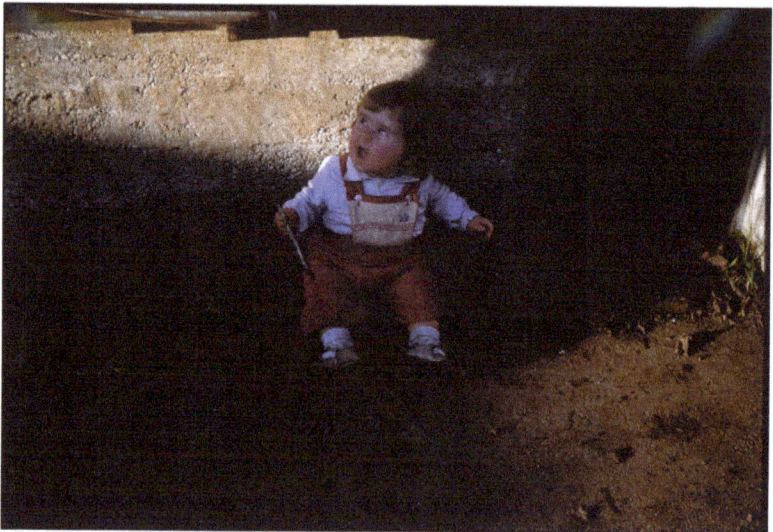

Scallywag (Christine) with a dripping tap

T his era, the 1960s, saw the advent of the 'Death of God' controversy. I could see the valid factors (the loss of *a sense of God* in the Western world) which the more substantial thinkers were daring to make public. J.B. Robinson's 'Honest to God' contained a lot of common sense. However, I could not even begin to entertain the Harvey Cox kind of uninhibited zest for the assumed liberations of 'The Secular City'.

Unlike some of my colleagues, I had never been able to give my soul to the safe but restrictive theology of Karl Barth. I had too much respect for that 'second Word of God', the natural world around us. It did not surprise me as this 'death of God' chatter really threw some Barthians and lead them to act rashly. The debate certainly put 'the frighteners' on many conservatives. The rumour that their Big Spook might have 'bought it' made them tremble and yell more loudly. I predicted at that time that there would be a reversion to simplistic, froth and bubble religion (such as happened within some of the early charismatic movement?) plus a rise in the popularity of the bizarre spirituality of the occult.

The book that had the biggest impact on me during those years was not a formal theological opus. The novel 'Christ Re-Crucified', by the famous Greek author Nikos Kazantzakis, got under my skin. His portrayal of a conflict between genuine discipleship and religious observance, and the rejection of fellow Greek refugees by the priest and 'good people' of the village, hit me between the eyes. About this time I became a devoted member of the simplicity-based organisation, 'Community Aid Abroad'.

Towards the end of my ministry in Glenorchy, the church was enlarged with the addition of a new and spacious sanctuary. The architect produced an inspiring result. Incidentally, the builder's name was Walker – the father of a certain youthful footballer and cricketer name Max.

During our stay on the hillside at Rosetta, overlooking the banks of the Derwent River, our family became supporters of the Glenorchy football team. The hardest thing was getting used to the club colours of black and white. Yes, they were indeed the colours of the 'Magpies'. For a long-time supporter of the Melbourne Football Club's red and blue, this was a hard pill for me to swallow.

David and Martin managed to get into scrapes with boys from our area, especially with the bright sons of our wonderful neighbours, Kath and Wally Alexander. David became a 'natural' leg spin bowler, and at the school sports day, Martin persevered with characteristic doggedness to complete a one-mile run and earn points for his school house and the admiration of his headmaster.

Christine was spoilt by the older girls in our crescent and won the sprint race (yes, she truly did!) at the kindergarten's sports day at Glenorchy.

At first Marie, ever the mother, felt bereft when Christine started infant school, but in time, she found there were bonuses. She once more obtained her driver's licence and found pleasure and fitness under the regime of the Cazaly (yes a son of the legendary footballer) Fitness Centre in central Hobart. She especially enjoyed a growing friendship with the warm-hearted neighbours, Kath and Wally Alexander.

The large, many-roomed size of our parsonage proved to be both good news and bad news. The good news was that there was always accommodation for family and friends. The bad news was that some importunate, ministerial acquaintances would invite themselves and their families to stay with us while on a visit to Hobart. Our 'room with a view' was just too convenient. After one exhausting succession of such visits, Marie had to say no to our dear friends, Max and Bev Spry. For a hospitable soul like my wife, that was a painful thing to have to do.

My relaxation was to play cricket with the Glenorchy Church team in the Hobart churches' competition. A complication was that Saturday funerals were still in favour in some quarters. Occasionally on Saturdays, I conducted funerals at the Cornelian Bay Cemetery, with my black gown covering my cricket whites. I added an extra silent prayer to the liturgy: that my team's batting would not have collapsed and be all out before I made it back to the cricket pitch.

During my time in Glenorchy, the Holy Spirit confronted my rigid teetotal stance. Firstly, there was a wedding of delicate and difficult circumstances. At the reception, I blithely rejected a glass of wine and asked for some soft drink. The bride's mother was painfully embarrassed. There was no soft drink provided. That got through to me.

On a second occasion, I was called to Collinsvale where the wife of a youngish Dutch migrant had suddenly collapsed and died in the bathroom. The poor fellow was devastated. Yet he rose above his grief to offer me hospitality, pouring an ale for my refreshment. I said a thank you but no, I did not drink beer, resulting in acute embarrassment on the man's face. He hastily apologised and poured me a glass of fortified black current wine. The Spirit shouted at me: "Drink it, you insensitive, unloving, self-righteous fool." I did. From that day forward, I gave away my rigid teetotal attitude. I became a rare drinker; a much more difficult position than having a black and white approach.

One other change to my public persona happened. In a men's discussion group we happened upon a passage from Karl Barth in which he rejected clerical collars as a religious uniform. I asked the dozen fellows how they saw the clerical collar. Until then I had always worn the collar, rarely out of it; so convenient, no choosing of shirts or ties, and an instant introduction in hospitals, nursing homes or civic functions. Surprise! Eleven out of the twelve fellows all said that they found a clerical collar a barrier, which only the passage of time and better acquaintance could lower. My God! I did not want barriers! From that moment, I vowed to limit my use of the ecclesiastical black front and white collar. When my time was done at Glenorchy, I would never wear one again.

Invited ('called') to High Street Road, Mt. Waverley, in the metropolis of Melbourne, we left Glenorchy after five enriching years. Sad to leave some beautiful friends, including some choice Roman Catholic Priests (who turned on a lavish farewell meal for our family) yet all were excited at the prospect of being close to Marie's family in Victoria after 12 years.

Alanvale
1962

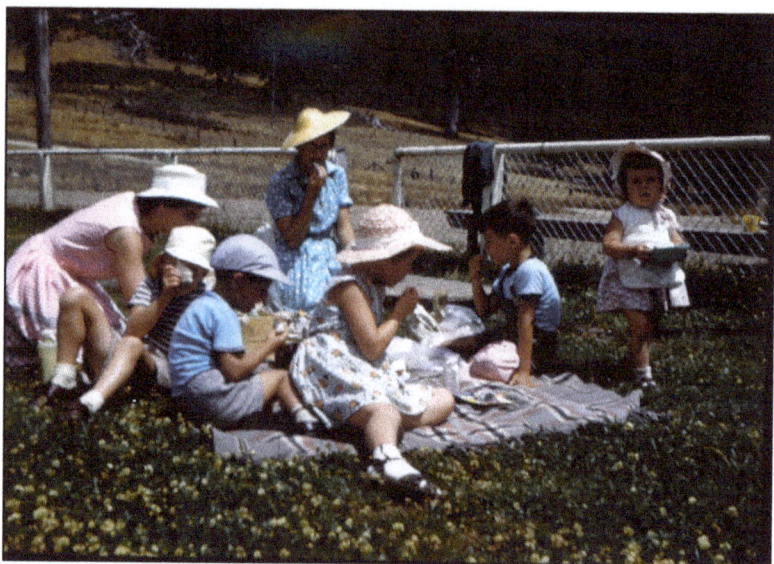

Above and below: Poatina
January 1962

David, Margaret, Andrew, Martin
Bridport, January 1962

Martin's 5th birthday
1962

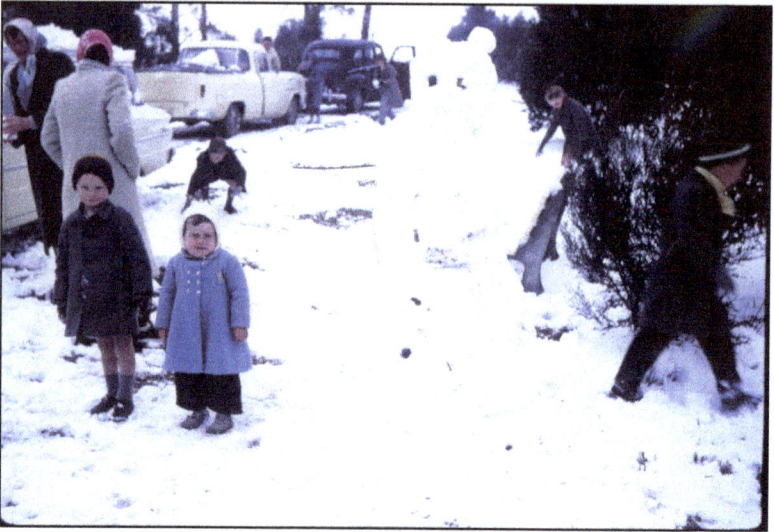

Margetts and Prewers
September 1962

Bridport near Old Pier
December 1962

Holidays
December 1962

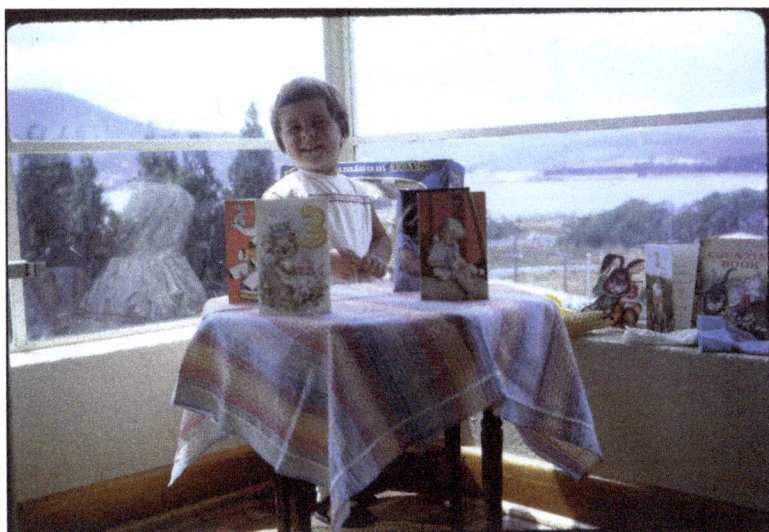

Christine Lyn Prewer's 3rd birthday
13th February 1963

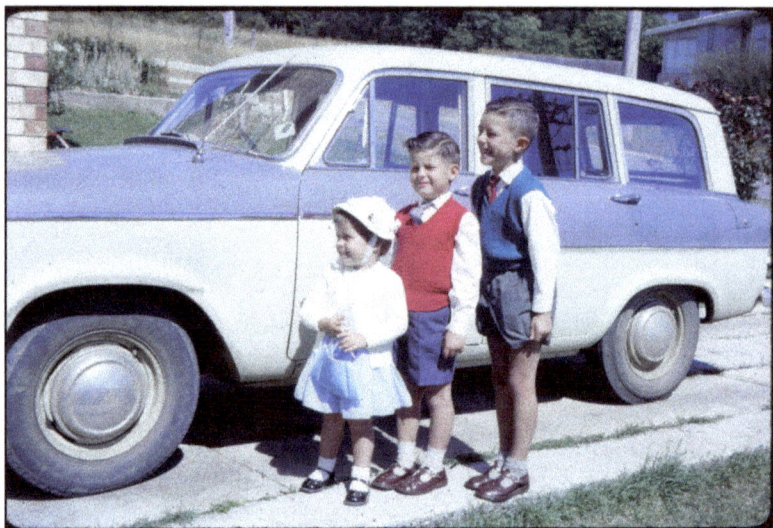

Off to Sunday School
February 1963

David, Martin and Christine
Mother's Day 1963

Christine and teddy in new pyjamas
13th February 1964

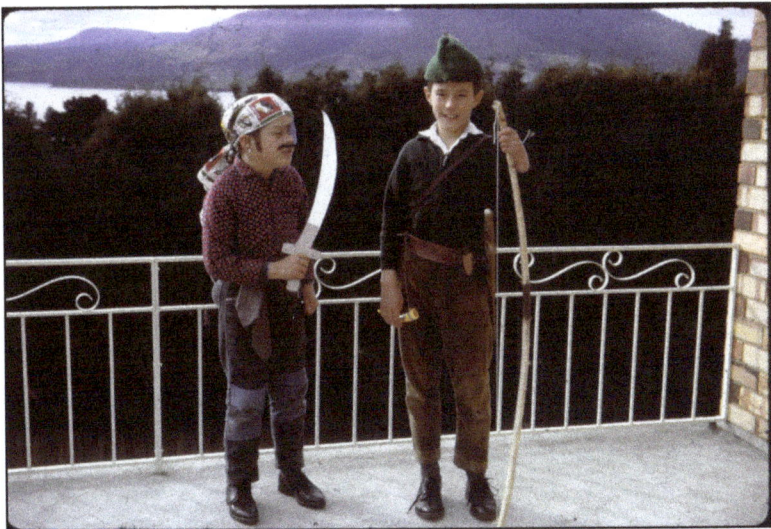

Book Week, Rosetta State School
1964

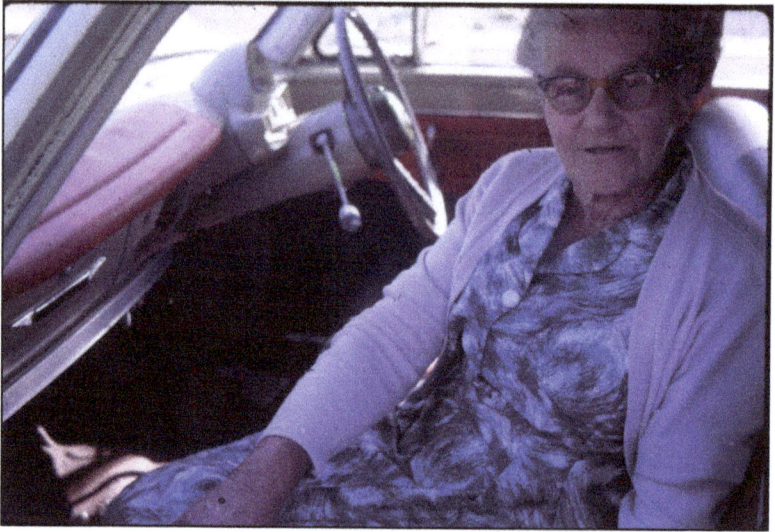

Grandma Prewer (Florrie), Cadbury's Point
April 1964

October 1964

Playmates at Lorraine Crescent
1964

Melbourne Zoo
January 1965

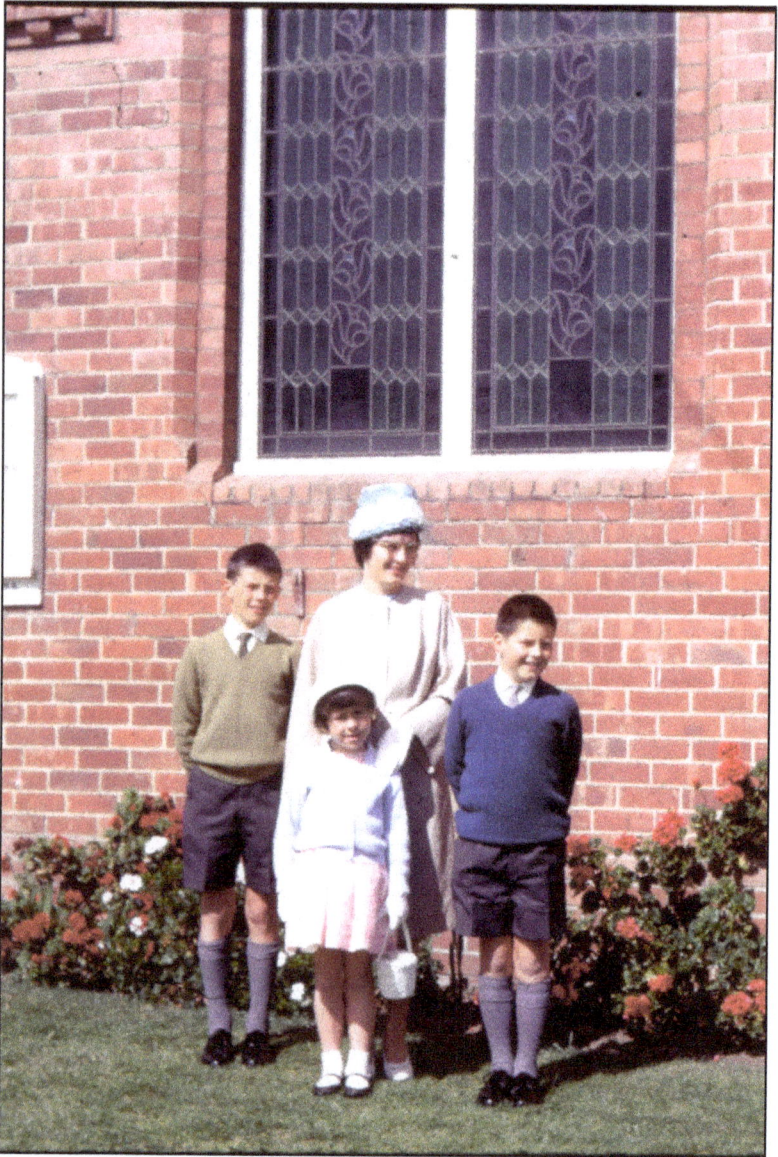

Glenorchy Methodist Church

BULGING AT THE SEAMS

MT. WAVERLEY – HIGH STREET ROAD: 1967-1973

In January 1967 we arrived in the wake of a furniture van at the parsonage in Stewart Street, next to the High Street Road Methodist Church, outer Melbourne. Thumbs up soon came from our three offspring! It had big grounds, plenty of space for the boys (and Christine!) to kick a football and play cricket.

This appointment would prove to be one of the most stimulating yet at times frightening, wonderful though painful, fruitful yet exhausting, congregations with whom I was able to share ministry. I say 'share ministry' because most of the numerous, gifted lay leaders had a firm grasp of the mission of the whole people of God. Many exciting things happened without yours truly having to lift a finger. What a joy it was to be carried along, rather than fearing I had do most of the carrying or pushing.

This did not mean the minister had a leisurely life. Far from it. Many people needed my backing in their work, others needed counselling, some wanted to bounce ideas off me. Time-wise and emotionally, I was as involved as ever. Maybe more so.

My pastorate was one corner of the large Burwood Circuit, with the Superintendent Minister being the pint-sized, big-hearted, stentorian-voiced Wilf Manzony, stationed at Warrigal Road. How I loved that man! I had others colleagues; Ron Yeats at East Burwood, Arthur Ellemore at Glen Waverley, and Bruce Richards, followed by the very gifted Ron Croxford, at Virginia Street Mt. Waverley. All had large congregations and Sunday Schools.

High Street Road was no exception. A full house at 9.30am and 11am (a superb choir at this second service) and a smaller yet steady congregation at 7pm. The Sunday School had over 450 children on the roll with an average attendance of about 250. Funerals were mercifully few but baptisms were multiple, celebrated once a month at both morning services. The largest number I baptised in one go was 12 babies.

A key area each Sunday was the large foyer linking church, Sunday School and meeting rooms. There we mixed and had morning tea, and kept in touch with each other's joys and sorrows. For special services (with the adjacent church windows fully open) we packed into this same foyer the overflow congregation. I said after a couple of years at this church: "If I were building a new complex, the first thing erected should be the foyer."

There were always exciting lay education programs running concurrently with one of the other services, also specific programs during the week. Never any shortage of stimulation and nurture. And joy of joys, not much of it was of my doing!

I did help initiate an in-depth review of our worship practices. As a result, the 9.30am congregation pioneered an informal, talkback style service. It included (maybe one of the first in Australia) open sharing times of joys and sorrows, baptisms held in the very centre of the congregation, much lay leadership and innovative prayers and litanies.

The 11am service remained more formal, but with me leading, one never knew exactly what new happening might take place. On one occasion, during Lent, a young dancer-in-training danced the theme of the Gospel while it was being read. A survey at the end of the program showed that over 80% of the congregation still recalled each Gospel reading.

The Leaders' Meeting took a take a brave step (for that stage of Methodist history) and invited all baptised children to participate in Holy Communion. On the first Sunday this was implemented at the 11am service, afterwards one lively, redheaded 10-year-old came to me and said: "Bruce, for the first time today I felt I really belonged in this church. What work can I now do to help?" He was soon made an assistant door steward and usher, and sometimes an offering steward, a task he relished.

Later in my life, as I have reflected on the possible reasons for the vigour of that congregation, I reached some conclusions.

Firstly, the original Methodists in the region, which had been a market garden and orchard region before the extensive housing estates arrived, did not resent the arrival of the avalanche of newcomers but gave them both a welcome and positions of authority and trust within the burgeoning congregation. Wonderful folk, such as the Lechte and Hore families, were two examples of this big-hearted, open-minded approach.

Secondly, the 'mother church' at Warrigal Road willingly shouldered the financial burden of assisting the work of God to grow and build new, or enlarge existing, worship centres. Without this, their young congregations may well have foundered.

Thirdly, the congregation was gifted with some choice, dedicated lay leadership, such as Bob Pepperell, Russ Hore, Shirley and Gorden Lovel, Bea Gunn, Ivan and Elsie Wilson, Jack and Sid Brown, Ken Turner, Ross and Maree Delbridge, Vern Wilkinson, Tony Michele, just to name a few. Apologies to the many others who could just as easily have been mentioned. We were amazingly blessed with the quality of these Christian souls.

Prior to our arrival, it had been decided that a new parsonage would be built. The present one was damp and mildew was common in bedrooms and wardrobes. Our

predecessors had suffered continuous ailments. As the
Melbourne and Metropolitan Board of Works would not
accept the proposition that there was leakage from their large,
closely adjoining reservoir, the Burwood Circuit had decided
to build a new house elsewhere. I tried to convince Wilf
Manzony that maybe inducted floor heating would solve the
problem. No go. "We won't put more good money after bad,
son." So after two years we moved to 75 Headingley Road, a
fine home with a view to the distant city and even (on a fine
day) to the You Yangs.

While at Mt. Waverley, Marie Joyce resumed her profession
as a nurse by working in a doctor's surgery at nearby Glen
Waverley. After a couple of years, she returned to her first
passion, serving as a midwife at the Jessie McPherson Hospital
in Lonsdale Street. Although she had butterflies in her
stomach, she soon settled back in and loved dealing again with
mums and babies. She did night duty, not the perfect answer,
but it suited our family routines the best. Moreover, it made
the children and me more keenly aware of the time and effort
required for housework and preparing meals. I took up a bit of
the slack and the kids added a few new duties to their lives.

David and Martin graduated from Primary School to
Mt. Waverley High School. There, our sons made a name for
themselves as capable students. David excelled at sports,
especially athletics and football, and Martin became keen on
cricket. Christine won a scholarship to Cato Methodist Ladies

College at Elsternwick. In addition, David learned to play classical guitar, Martin the clarinet and Christine the flute.

By example, I (so it seems) indoctrinated the family into becoming supporters of the Melbourne Football Club. Many Saturday afternoons saw us at one of the grounds cheering the lowly red and blue. We usually watched our team lose and then returned home religiously to a meal of fish and chips.

Our family finance was tight. The real value of the stipend had been slipping behind inflation for some years. To this day we are grateful that our three kids never complained or made us feel bad about their relative (compared to most of their peers) poverty. We drew up a yearly budget that had to be strictly adhered to. One year I handed a copy to a member of the Conference 'Stipends Review Committee'. He was shocked. With my permission, he shared it with the members of that Committee. They had never before sat down and worked out the details of what could actually be done with such a stipend. With the warm backing of the Chair of the Committee, the banker-economist Brian Hambly, things steadily improved after that.

Toward the end of our seven years at High Street Road, much ministerial and lay energy went into dialogue with the Syndal Presbyterian Church, whose minister was the loveable Fred Strickland.

They too had some excellent lay leaders among their Elders. Things went well and a few years before the UCA came into being, a united congregation was ready to be formed.

As the counselling load increased, I sharpened my skills by undertaking a two-year, part-time course in clinical pastoral counselling. This made me more aware that my own emotional health was failing (or fraying!) Bone weary at times, all adrenalin drained, anxiety levels up to nine or ten, even over mini matters, I increased my meditation quota and read more books in the field. It helped, but not enough. I became more volatile and anger-prone with Marie and the kids. I was in severe inner distress and pain and did not know how to handle the angst.

After one scary day, with Marie away in the city and the kids at school, I just sat as if paralysed for seven hours at my desk, doing nothing at all until school was out and the children's voices sounded at the back door. Things could not go on like this.

I made an appointment with an eminent psychiatrist and committed Methodist layman, Dr. Don Oldmeadow. He heard me out through a long hour and then claimed I was suffering from severe depression. I argued. No way, I knew myself! I had an acute anxiety condition, not depression. He calmly shook his head. I finally agreed to go on medication for a month (he explained that it would take at least two weeks before the benefits would begin to appear). If over four weeks there was no improvement, he might retract his diagnosis.

The next few weeks were horrible. The medication made it difficult to keep awake. My speech was thick. Sermons had to be laboriously prepared and slowly read aloud word for word.

In retrospect, I should have been placed on sick leave. God alone knows what the congregations thought I was up to, but the medical miracle slowly happened. In a few weeks, my anxiety and angst subsided. I became more mood-moderate and able again. Not a 100% result, but much improved. Don Oldmeadow was right. I had been wrong. As with most mental and emotional illness, the subject can rarely analyse himself.

Two study books were published during these hectic years: *The Freedom to Become* and *It's Hard to Love Your Neighbour.*

L ater the next year, Marie and I took three months' long service leave plus a month accrued annual leave. We farmed the kids out to kindly parishioners and flew out of Tullamarine with my cousin Vere Hazelwood and his wife Allison, camping for three months around Israel, Europe and Scandinavia, followed by one month of touring around the UK. What a joy all that exploring (no, not *all* but *most* of it) was for us, and what marvellous mid-life bonding for our marriage.

I was especially impressed and moved by the hundreds of sculptures in Oslo by Gustav Vigeland. These featured and celebrated common people. We returned home seeing ourselves and our homeland and culture in a new light. I had previously dabbled in writing distinctly Australian prayers, but now I was determined to work harder at it.

During those seven years at Mt. Waverley, I became too heavily involved in central church committees and made many out-of-parish visits as a speaker at seminars. I was elected to the Victoria-Tasmania Conference Standing Committee and the General Conference, Secretary of the Theological Hall, member of the Board of Christian Citizenship Department, Ministerial Candidates Committee and a lot of other sub-committee stuff. I also became an elected member of the Methodist General Conference of Australia and of a couple of its commissions. Stupid man! Flattered by seeming to be so wanted (note: not *needed*) I just did not know how to say 'no'.

Finally when was I confined to bed for a week with a gastro infection that would not let me go, Marie (bless her sanity!) made me sign a statement "I Bruce Prewer, being of sound mind, promise to immediately remove myself from Standing Committee and such others whenever my elected term expires. I promise to take more time off and exercise my body as well as my mind." I followed through with much of that promise and resigned from the Standing Committee of the Vic-Tas Conference, phased myself out from others and took up some jogging and a little bushwalking with Marie in those nearby hills and mountains known simply as 'the Dandenongs'.

At the end of seven years, the annual Stationing Committee moved us on to North Essendon. I went most reluctantly, having hoped for one extra year to see the Presbyterian and Methodist congregations fully merged at Mt. Waverley.

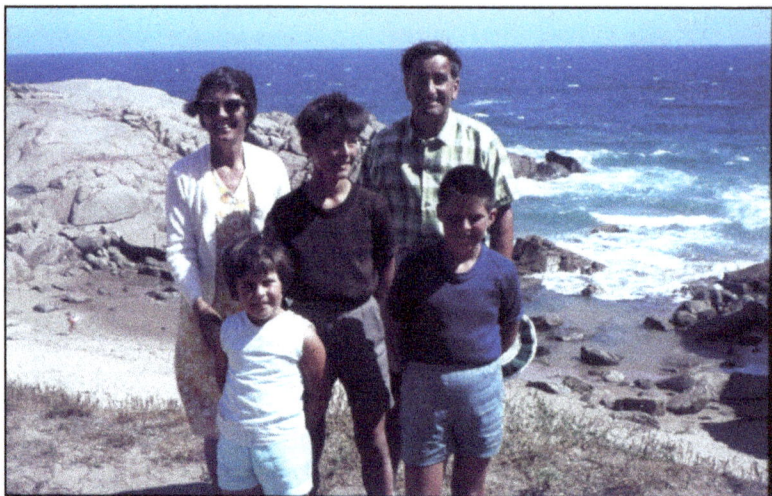

Victor Harbor, SA
January 1968

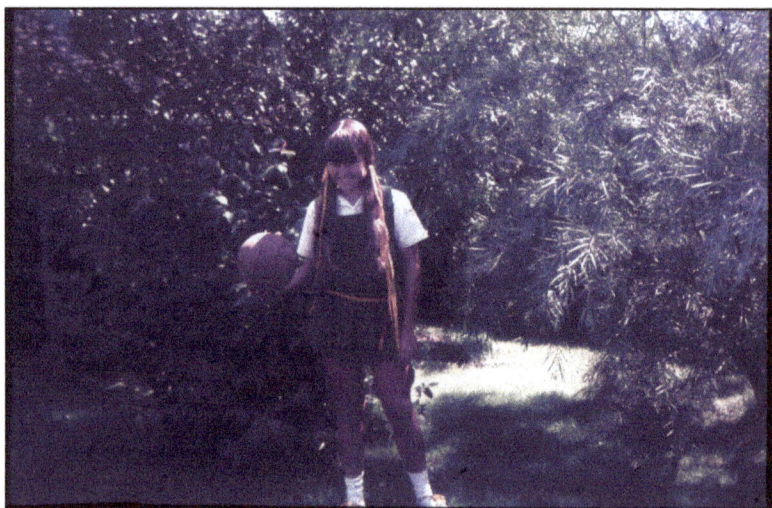

Chris, ready for Cato MLC House Sports
1973

Chris, 2nd from right, Cato MLC House Sports
1973

Campsite at Hattah Lakes
August 1974

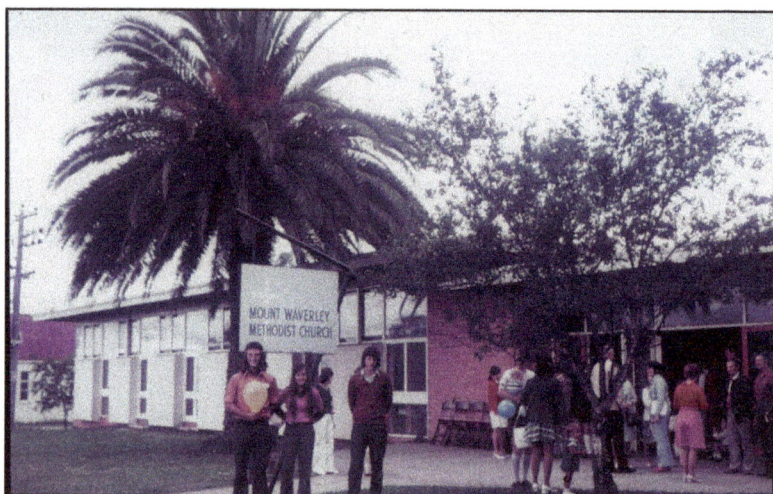

Last Service at Mt. Waverley
December 1973

NORTH ESSENDON

In 1974 we arrived at North Essendon, a church with a fine history, sited in the palm-tree-lined, Mt. Alexander Road. I followed the Rev. Doug Risstrom, a loveable preacher, pastor and an ex-President of our Conference.

For us it was a culture shock – a very traditional church, choir, worship and buildings that did not look to have altered in 50 years. There was still a Union Jack hanging over the pulpit and the elderly choir was centre stage, up front. Yet in that congregation were some of the most loving, perceptive Christians I have ever met: such as George and May Davidson, Gladys Newbold, Vi Morgan, Joy Tranter, Merle Hill, Margaret Graham, Frank and Jean Rosewarne, Vern and Hilary Kerton, Ray and Rosemary Leach, and others. However, Marie and I were among the few younger members of that congregation which had shrunk in 20 years (a changing demography) from about 300 to 80 loyal souls.

The North Essendon Circuit, of which I was now the Superintendent Minister, consisted of six churches and three ministers: Coralie Ling, Ron Yeats and me. Coralie, a strong yet non-abrasive feminist, helped me to journey much further down the road towards inclusive language in worship.

Church union was drawing closer. I worked extensively on various interim committees of the three denominations as they prepared for the change. Locally, the Presbyterian and Methodist parishes were coming together. It was exacting and draining work. Often I was monumentally tired but I believed church union was worth the pain. Much later, during the latter years of life, I have been known to comment: "There are a number things about the Uniting Church which are like gravel in my shoes. But if I had to live it all again, I would make the same journey."

A mighty help through this time were the gratis secretarial services offered by Vi McFarlane of the Aberfeldie Church. Without Vi's skills and work ethic, the secretarial load would have been too much for me.

At North Essendon, I experimented extensively at 'Australianising' the language of prayers and some of the Psalms. A little bit of this had been happening while at Mt. Waverley but now I gave this task a dedicated, daily focus. Some kindly souls, like George Davidson and Reg Young, gave me encouragement to continue.

Another of the happy aspects of this appointment was being able to work closely with Presbyterian ministers Robert Renton at Keilor Road and Bob Catford at St. John's. A special delight was Deaconess (and soon to be minister) Achera Brunelli and her husband (to be) Angelo; these two were a perfect soul-mix of Thai and Italian.

By now, David was at the University of Melbourne and Martin followed a year later. Christine continued at Cato College, Elsternwick, and then moved on to do a Bachelor of Education at Melbourne. Martin conscientiously worked through all university vacations and missed out on some family holidays, such as a visit to Perth and a stay in the University College named *Kingswood*, where an old friend, the Rev. Bill Ellis, was then the Master.

Marie continued night duty at the Jessie Mac. The excellent tram service to Essendon made the getting to and fro much simpler than it had been from Mt. Waverley.

In our 40s, Marie and I bought a double kayak and extended our love affair with water. For many years thereafter, holidays and days off included adventures on rivers, lakes and even in the ocean at Pt. Roadnight, Anglesea. As well, we were enthusiastic body surfers.

It was while we were living in the parsonage at 72 Richardson Street, that I re-encountered the many dimensions of orchestral music. Much improved stereo sound systems, which were then becoming more affordable, assisted me to transcend my long-term hearing difficulties. With the added

help of good quality earphones, I realised I could unscramble
the texture of orchestral works that had previously eluded me.
The result was I became addicted to classical music. I found
how well those genius composers like Bach, Beethoven and
Mozart, could capture spiritual hungers, fears and joys in a
way no words could ever express.

As the Uniting Church came into being, our region moved
to form one Essendon Parish, with five ministers and six
congregations. The Rev. Coralie Ling (ex-Methodist) continued
to minister to the congregations at Buckley Park and
Aberfeldie. The largest fellowship by far was that of the
ex-Presbyterian St. John's Church, cared for by Rev. Bob
Catford, Deaconess Achera Brunelli and before long joined
by the Rev. John Hudson. At the same time, Rev. Rob
Renton (ex-Presbyterian, Keilor Road)) and I (ex-Methodist,
Mt. Alexander Road) were encouraging a joint-committee as
they worked painstakingly at trying to combine our two
smaller congregations into one congregation at North
Essendon.

As a date drew near for a decision on combining our
worship and outreach at North Essendon, a few self-appointed
'patriots' in both congregations went around lobbying their
fellow members and stirring up new anxieties and reviving
old wounds. I (piously passive, I am now sorry to confess)
refrained from this 'politicking', urging Rob Renton to likewise
hold his fire and "let the Spirit do her work". The final phase
was a joint meeting of both congregations, chaired by our

Presbytery Officer, Rev. Brace Bateman. A series of votes was taken and counted and we awaited the result of the final count.

Failure. The two congregations would not be combining. The tricky question of which church property would be our future worship and fellowship centre was too much. The lobbyists had done their work well; it proved to be the one insurmountable hurdle. The attachment to properties overwhelmed the desire to become one congregation. It hurt Rob and me deeply to see our two congregations so openly 'shafting' each other during that series of ballots.

I was both disappointed and angry. Very angry at myself for piously refusing to take part in any pastoral 'politicking'. Angry at those lay folk who shamelessly did so, and angry at the many who, in that joint meeting of congregations, openly shafted each other. I did not feel I could go on ministering to congregations who had proved to be addicted to what I truly believed was idol worship – edifice idolatry.

The next Sunday I felt compelled to make a stand, but how and what could I really do? First, I contacted my psychiatrist to see if he thought this was an aberration of my depression or medication. He thought not. Then I spoke with my colleagues, laying before them the 'nuts and bolts' of what I was intending. They gave me some feedback and I amended my plans somewhat.

The following Sunday I made what I considered to be a valid prophetic protest against 'structural heresy'. I clothed myself in rough hessian and preached a notorious sermon on the seductive yet crumbling nature of all our structural idols. I did not hide my anger – at my overly-pious self, at those self-appointed lobbyists, and at what many members so openly did to each other that previous Sunday. I then said I could no longer be a faithful minister of the Gospel in such a deviant situation.

(Only the Holy Spirit knows how close to being 'right' or 'wrong' I really was. Had my words and deeds been the best thing I could to do in that situation? Or was I being a like a child in a tantrum, spitting the dummy when I did not get my way? Over 30 years on and I still do not know for certain whether I was truly being the Lord's servant that day, or not.)

Maybe I had taken myself too seriously during those turbulent days. A couple of weeks later, one night at about 1.30am, I ended up in the ICU at the Royal Melbourne with an agonising heart seizure. Pastoral care guru, Prof. Graeme Griffin, paid me a visit the following day. He put his finger on the salient point "Don't leave this place, Bruce, without answering 'What lessons about myself have I learnt from this experience?' " Thank you, wise and caring Graeme.

One thing was certain. I had burnt my own bridges. I had surely rendered myself unemployed and maybe unemployable in the wider church.

Meanwhile, my colleagues Bob Catford, Coralie Ling, Achera Brunelli, John Hudson and Robert Renton took up the slack caused by my turbulence. To them I owed considerable thanks for their care, especially to John Hudson who covered for me at North Essendon.

While all this was taking place, my struggle against chronic depression continued; maybe it was aggravated by utter weariness and too much miss-spent adrenalin. I had sought more counselling from a guy who was supposed to be one of Victoria's best psychiatrists. After some months of analysis, he had uncovered little to work on and concluded mine was an authentic case of 'endogenous' depression. He did change my medication to one *Nardil* that helped me immensely, yet he warned me it could have drastic side effects (brain haemorrhage or heart seizure) if taken with alcohol and certain foods such as cheese, beans or yeast-extract products. That made me somewhat edgy when eating out.

A bright spot near the end of 1979 was the publication of a new, poetic book bearing my name. My first volume of prayers with a definitive Aussie flavour, was produced by the Lutheran Publishing House in Adelaide. I first viewed it while in the coronary ward at the Royal Melbourne. I was astounded when *Australian Psalms* became a religious best seller in Australia and was regarded as newsworthy overseas. A few expat colleagues mailed me newspaper clippings from abroad.

I did not fully realise it then, but I had evidently pioneered what one publishing guru some years later told me was 'a new, distinctly Australian way to talk with God'. Many have now followed the trend, some producing creative liturgical resources much more skilled than my efforts. Some are in fact brilliant. (Beware, dear Bruce, the 'green monster'!) Tinges of envy aside, to be a participant in worship when such innovative, Aussie-style liturgies created by others are being used, gives me the most profound satisfaction and gratitude to the Sister Spirit of all creativity.

Throughout August and September 1979, I was somewhat anxious. What would my future be? We doubted that any parish would ever want my services, in light of my actions (be they read as disconcertingly prophetic or a mere dummy spit) at North Essendon. Maybe some rural parish might take me on? But it was just as well I did not hold my breath waiting. When I attended the annual Synod of the church held in St. Michael's, Collins Street Melbourne, in October, no parish had showed any interest in calling me.

What other form of employment could I possibly engage in? Although my depression was being well held back by the new medication regime, my future looked decidedly grey.

A NEW BEGINNING

C ompletely out of the blue came a letter from the city of Adelaide. My name was on the top of a short list to be considered for their two-person, collegiate ministry at Pilgrim Church, in the city centre. The other minister, already in settlement, was the affable Rev. Grant Dunning.

I knew little about Pilgrim Church, except that it was the result of an amalgamation of the congregations of a central Methodist and a nearby Congregational church. That fact impressed me. They had already taken and implemented the painful decision that our two churches at North Essendon had balked at.

While preparing a CV, I talked a lot with Marie, and also with other ministers who were more familiar with the character of Pilgrim Church. The now-retired and still ebullient Trevor Byrd, a previous minister at Pilgrim Church, who had worked assiduously to help bring the two congregations of Pirie Street Methodist and Stow Memorial together, was particularly helpful.

What of our own family? If we moved to another state, it would have big ramifications for our family. David was now working, Martin was doing a post-grad Social Work course, and 20-year-old Christine was still involved in her B. Ed. They, the darling offspring that they were (knowing it was the end of the family unit they had known from birth) sat tight on whatever grief and anxiety they were experiencing and gave us their full encouragement for us to consider this new option.

What of our own parents? They were becoming increasingly frail; we wondered about going further away from them. Jess and George Goldsmith, now living in retirement at Healesville and recently turned 80, were already living much closer to their son Ronald and daughter Jean than we were. Moreover, my parents Florrie and Cliff Prewer (both now entering their 90s) had their son Ray and daughter Dorothy living nearby, which quelled our anxiety on that score. Besides, they would still be only one short plane flight away.

Once clear of our annual UCA Synod, we agreed to drive to Adelaide and be interviewed by the Selection Committee at Pilgrim, and to chat with my prospective colleague, the Rev. Grant Dunning. I did not want them to be under any illusion about my track record. I discussed with the members of that Committee the sudden, somewhat bizarre, termination of my ministry at North Essendon, and my subsequent heart seizure. It did not seem to put them off at all. To the contrary, they seemed even keener on calling this clerical gadfly.

That visit left made me convinced that the hand of the Holy One was in this. Marie Joyce concurred with that impression. Back at North Essendon, we were not at all surprised when a unanimous call arrived in the mail. Adelaide, an amiable city of about a million souls, was not the modest rural, centre that Marie and I had anticipated, but the Spirit does not abide by our human plans. Without hesitation, I wrote back with an unequivocal "Yes!"

We agreed to commence at Pilgrim in August 1980. Although I was eager to get started in Adelaide, I chose to delay that move until after the Rev. Bob and Val Catford had taken three months' long service leave, leaving me to care for St. John's Church, Essendon. That interim ministry proved to be a bonus for me. Their hearty encouragement and enthusiasm for my ministry during that short period helped heal both my physical body and the emotional ulcer of self-doubt which had hampered me after what I saw as my abject failure at North Essendon. By the grace of God, I was being readied for the next big challenge.

With Marie's highly-strung, snow-white cat, Kunama, sedated in a basket, we hugged goodbye David, Martin and Christine on a cold, windy morning at the end of July and drove off for the City of Adelaide in our small Datsun 180B, our kayak on the roof and a small *Sunbird* caravan in tow. At the rural city of Horsham, we stopped for a welcome lunch with our long-time friends, the Rev. Alan and Marj Collins.

That evening, after a difficult and at times hazardous 11-hour drive, we parked in a 'pull off' in the Adelaide Hills, peered through the rain at the city lights far below and committed our future into the bountiful hands of God. Half an hour later, the rugged little Datsun 180B, with kayak still on its roof-bars and caravan attached, got us to the manse at Toorak Gardens, not on schedule but safely, by 8pm that evening.

Pilgrim Church, Adelaide, 1980-1989

We loved our new environment. The manse in Toorak Gardens was spacious, surrounded by a native garden, and was situated only 10 minutes from Pilgrim Church in Flinders Street, near Victoria Square.

A week later, our dear friends Bruce and Shirley Rollins drove from Ballarat to Adelaide for our induction. Bruce, no longer himself a minister, presented me with a new edition of the Bible, inscribed simply with the words "The Word became flesh". If only that could become true for me in this new ministry.

The saintly (truly so but never in her own eyes) Rosalie McCutcheon, and the Parish Council Secretary – the smiling Chris Ward, together with the Rev. Grant Dunning, shared with Synod dignitaries in leading my induction service. My erstwhile mentor, the now retired Rev. Guv Inglis, preached the 'charge'.

In the Induction Service, we received our first taste of the most wonderful choir a pastor could ever pray for. I was to soon discover that the organist-choirmaster, the renowned musician David Merchant, could be a cantankerous maestro, but he always made sure the choir set it sights on the highest quality possible. God be praised!

Grant Dunning had a natural and well-honed gift for traditional liturgy. I was able to observe, listen and learn much from him. We formed truly a collegiate team.

We were very blessed in that congregation, with the encouragement of numerous, very gifted, ordained ministers. *Retired ministers:* Bill Curry, Arthur Johnson, Dwight Large (ex USA Methodist), Maurie Wilmshurst, Ken Leaver, Guv Inglis, Bruce Trigg, Dr. Jock Barrie, Geoff Drake, Gordon Moyle and Ray Nixon. Those working in *Specialist Ministries:* lecturers Dr. Laurie Mickan and Dr. Vic Hayes, Clinical Psychologist Dr. Geoff Pope, the Master of Lincoln University College Dr. John Whitehead, his successor Dr. Geoff Scott, *Chaplains* – Dr. Alan Farr, William Dow, John Edwards, Duncan Morris, Peter Holden and *poet/teacher* Dr. Don Bell.

Looking at those names and their elite abilities, one might wonder if they were a threat to the two pastors in settlement? No way. I cannot emphasise enough how unobtrusively those numerous ministers fitted in. They gave my colleague and me their discerning support, overlooking our deficiencies and where appropriate, backing us with their respective gifts. Guv, Maurie and Alan especially became models for me in my own later retirement.

I had made up my mind that in Adelaide I would eschew Synod committees and focus on using my stronger abilities to the full as pastor, preacher, innovative liturgist and enabler. The only regular wider-church commitment was on the board of the UCA press where I was privileged to know and appreciate gifted editors like Tony Nancarrow (a founder of MediaCom) and David Busch (later an ABC National talkback host).

Pilgrim was a busy place, all days of the week. On Sundays, there were morning services at 8am (always Holy Communion followed by a simple breakfast), 9.30am (informal, extensive lay input) and 11am (formal and choral). Evening Prayers were at 7pm and weekday Eucharists were celebrated on Tuesday at 8am and Thursdays at 12.10pm. The comfortable lounge and kitchen at the rear of the church were open each day of the week for anyone to have a cuppa or a chat with one of our lovely volunteer staff.

Being a central church, along with the cathedrals and other city churches such as Flinders Street Baptist and Bethlehem Lutheran, we took our ecumenical turn in hosting annual civic services such as those of the Legal Profession, Australia Day, British Commonwealth Day, and various community organisations like the Red Cross and the Hearing Impaired Association.

Pilgrim was blessed with fine musicians. David Merchant at the organ was truly awesome. Moreover, he had drawn into his excellent choir those four singers known for years on ABC National Radio as 'The Adelaide Singers'. Genty, Vivian, Malcolm and Noel were the 'principal' soloists, who with the other choir members often had me in tears, especially with their rendition of the Psalm set for each Sunday. The 9.30 community had the extrovert composer and pianist, Dr. Doug Simper, to head the musical side of things, Norm Inglis as required on the pipe organ, and quality singers like Dr. Graeme McIntosh and Lorna Xzulan, to add highlights.

Having such an excellent choir meant that the religious department of the ABC was at times interested in either televising or broadcasting worship from Pilgrim Church. This was a privilege, yet it was also an exacting business. After one such ABC event, a choir member commented to me: "When I become nervous, I look down at your smiling, serene face, Bruce, and that relaxes me." Little did she know how frantically that ministerial 'black swan' was paddling under the water. To paraphrase a line from an old hymn, "behind a smiling countenance he hides an anxious gut".

For most of my nine years at Pilgrim, the church was open each day for people to slip in for quiet reflection or prayer. This facility was well used by many, most of whom were not members of our congregations. There, in the serenity of that beautiful and historic sanctuary, I experienced unforgettable encounters with dear souls in their hour of crisis. A few years later, after two attempts by vandals to set fire to our heritage building, the front doors had to be closed, leaving a side entrance available. Regretfully, following further vandalism, all the outer church doors had to be locked. Nowadays, when worship is not happening, the only entry is via the public lounge.

Always there was much pastoral work and counselling to be done. We were not the kind of ministers who stayed put in the centre of the city and waited for folk to come to us. Each Tuesday, at our staff meeting, we would review the list of the sick and frail. Each minister would accept responsibility for visiting them, across many suburbs and in numerous hospitals and nursing homes. Maurie Wilmshurst, and later Ken Leaver, gave us substantial assistance in this pastoral work. Most counselling was by appointment, although if we happened to be on-site at the time when enquirers entered the lounge, we would have fruitful, ad hoc, pastoral encounters "with all sorts and conditions of men".

Weddings took up copious time. My record was five weddings on one Saturday. We would not conduct a wedding ceremony without the couple first undertaking pre-marriage counselling. Soon I enlisted the help of lay counsellors for the congregations. After these became trained and qualified, they capably led hundreds of couples through an excellent preparation course. This not only lightened the load on the ministers, but also provided a quality, pre-marriage counselling service.

The people of Pilgrim were diverse in background gifts, personalities and their private needs. One member summed it up during our first month at Pilgrim: "You will discover that many of us are refugees from suburban churches for one reason or another." There was occasional tension between members of the informal 9.30 community, and the formal, 'high church' worship at 11am. The minister's role was to minister to all groups without fear or favour. That included a sizable group of gifted, caring gay members.

On the staff of Pilgrim were dedicated lay folk June Grey (administrator), Phil Kilgaur (typist/secretary) and Ray Beanland (verger).

June gave her utmost plus – a totally committed servant of Christ, who after a difficult childhood, made a treasured contribution to family and church. June was invaluable to me in my early days with her comprehensive knowledge of things 'Adelaide-ian'. Nothing was too much trouble. Yet June could on occasion herself be a 'handful' in that she took too many matters to heart and fretted herself sick. Likewise, her inappropriate 'need to know' all things pastoral, became chronic. Marie and I loved June dearly and respected her much more than she could ever comprehend.

Ray, the verger, was a buoyant bonus (cordial to visitors, willing to give extra time and cash to the beautification of the church and its mighty organ, and a competent pianist and organist) yet he became a law unto himself. As I have observed with other caretakers, in time Ray came to view the property as his personal fiefdom. Ray disliked the 9.30 community and made no secret of it, bad mouthing it occasionally to newcomers. He enjoyed thumbing his nose at authority, including officers of the SA Synod when they held regular evening meetings in the Pilgrim lounge.

Later on, my colleague Grant Dunning, a lifelong friend of Ray, commented: "He has to go." That proved a little messy to achieve. His departure (to St. Peter's Anglican Cathedral) was the loss of one of Pilgrim's best assets and yet also the removable of one of its most irksome irritants.

Grant and his wife Joy were a major support to us throughout those early months and years of our sojourn in Adelaide. Their intimate knowledge of the city, and of both the gifts and foibles of people in the church, were invaluable.

For the first five years (or was it six?) my duties included being chaplain to Annesley College, a major UCA girls' school. Pilgrim was the church which the 'boarders' attended each Sunday. Being chaplain involved me in leading worship in a full assembly at 9am each Wednesday morning and, with Marie Joyce at my side, dining one evening a week with the boarders. We were available to give counsel should one of the girls seek it. It was a happy, although at times, an awkward ministry. I was not a participant in the decision-making, power structures of the school, yet I did my best to play a significant role in caring for the students. Eventually I encouraged a newly appointed headmistress to work towards obtaining a full time chaplain.

After two years in the manse in Toorak Gardens, we put a deposit on our own home and moved to the hillside suburb of Magill. It was our plan to get a toehold in the property market, so that we would not be 'caught short' when we finally came to retirement. I built a study in the second garage, and so we settled neatly into our first ever, private home in 1983.   Its swimming pool was a bonus during Adelaide's long scorching summers. The red grape vines in the back garden were prolific. This change to an outer suburb did mean we needed a second car. We purchased a small red Honda, which became a favourite of mine.

Marie and I looked forward to regularly having Christine across for the long Uni vacs, and later during school holidays, from her first teaching position at the Mallee school of Manangatang. David, a qualified computer wizard, had gone off to England to pursue his own dreams. Martin was by now a busy social worker employed in the inner suburb of North Melbourne.

Martin and his lovely and artistic girlfriend (a school teacher named Lynne Waddingham) became engaged. On the 6th January 1983, I had the honour of taking a leading part in their wedding ceremony in the Buckley Park Church, still within the Essendon parish. A memorable day it certainly was;

a sweltering 40°C, with black ash falling on the wedding party from bush fires as far away as Ballan.

To crown the excitement, during the service I found out (in a whispered conversation with the bridegroom during the singing of a hymn) that Martin had accidentally left the wedding ring in a sponge bag in the boot of their car. The matter demanded quick thinking. During the Bible readings, I moved down from the sanctuary and sat beside Marie in the front pew. ("How nice and companionable," thought my sister, Dorothy, sitting nearby.) Surreptitiously, I wrested the ring from my wife's finger. Lynne was almost certainly the only bride wedded in that church to be married with her mother-in-law's ring. As they were later signing the certificates, I slipped out and procured from their vehicle the correct ring, much to Lynne's relief.

While in Adelaide, Marie studied at the Sturt campus for a Diploma of Applied Science in Nursing. She qualified with Honours. She also was elected as an elder by the 9.30am congregation (in 'her own right' – the nominees were adamant – not as a sop to a minister's wife!)

For recreation, Marie Joyce went to yoga and spent regular, happy Thursdays with a secular walking group, tramping the hills and valleys around Adelaide. For a time she nursed in the 'mid ward' at the Northern Hospital.

My emotional health remained stable for the first two years at Pilgrim. However, when our son David, now engaged to Nancy (a pharmacist in England) was to be married in Stonehouse, Gloucestershire, I, metaphorically speaking, 'shot myself in the foot'. Worried about travelling overseas and risking the grim health dangers posed by my medication, I sought a change.

I had to find a new psychiatrist and to trust his judgment. Our GP referred me. This new 'shrink' changed my medication for a safer, but unusual one. It proved barely adequate; left me existing between the narrow confines of two horizontal planes, set only a few notches above severe depression. On my worst days, my mood-level sat only a whisker over absolute zero.

Late in November, we flew out on a hot Adelaide day of 38°C, and 34 hours later, we arrived in London with it at 7°C. Nancy proved to be a vivacious delight. Our first-born son certainly had this decision right.

In their old VW camper whimsically christened 'Vince', David and Nancy took us exploring Devon and Cornwall in deep mid-winter, including searching for the birthplace of some of my ancestors, the Pearn family. We located it in a deep, damp, freezing valley where squatted the hamlet of Herodsfoot. We were not left wondering why Henry Davis Pearn, the father of my sombre grandmother, Annie Prewer, gathered up his wife and three children, leaving that gloomy hollow in 1857 to make his way to Plymouth, and from there took sail on the long and tedious voyage for far-flung Australia.

Christine, and then Martin and Lynne, arrived in the UK for their brother's wedding. We went tripping off with them (first with Chris, later with Martin and Lynne) to locate the Breckland region in Norfolk and Suffolk, from where the Prewer family had migrated; also from whence, one generation later, Marie's grandfather, George Harvey Goldsmith, had lived as a boy before moving to the cotton mills of Lancashire. We also visited the Lincoln town of Hucknall, the town where my mother's father, Walter Wheat, had toiled as a child labourer in a coal mine before he migrated to Australia.

Back in Gloucestershire, with typical, generous English hospitality, the Rev. Frank Thixton and his dear wife vacated their parsonage to allow our family to be together on the night before David's marriage. I was chuffed to be asked to share with Frank Thixton in the marriage ceremony. It snowed a little later on that auspicious day, which made it more romantic for the tribe of antipodeans Prewers. Following the celebrations, Marie Joyce and I flew to Spain for a week's self-drive tour in Andalusia, before returning home to another heatwave in Adelaide.

My anxiety and angst were now unremitting. The psychiatrist argued I was doing well enough, and fool that I was, I trusted him. Each day was a 'grit-the-teeth-and-get-on-with-it' kind of experience. I have vivid memories of staring into the bathroom mirror each morning trying to remember what one had to do with a face in order to make it smile. I had to practise before every public, up-front duty. The result, I fear, was more like an unsavoury leer.

My book of *Australian Prayers* was published in 1983. It took an enormous effort to pose for one adequate photo for the press. Yet the public reception of this volume was enthusiastic! The one major South Australian newspaper ran a banner headline on its front page. The overseas press picked up the story. No better book launch could be imagined.

My mood should have been jubilant. Not so. My chronic depression, allied to the unsuitable medication I was on, gave me no leave for high spirits. Things were grim. If my mood level was to be scored out of ten (0 = suicidal anguish, 10 = sweet optimism, above 10 = manic) then mine would fluctuate between 2 and 5. I felt trapped between those two constricting planes.

One thing that did help was taking most Mondays off and bush walking with Marie in the Adelaide Hills. That time with her usually lifted my mood level up near the top of its now limited range.

It was only my profound sense of having been *called* to the ministry that kept me going. I fought like a tiger to be a good pastor and preacher to the best of my ability. Each day I claimed faith over against all that was negative. I refused to be ruled by my feelings. Like the turbulent Martin Luther, I threw many an imaginary ink well at the smirking devils and shouted "I am baptised. You go to hell!"

Ever since I first gave my life to God of Christ, the interval I had set aside for morning prayer and meditation was essential. For me, prayer at evenings is useless; I soon nod off into slumber. Apart from occasional unavoidable circumstances, I have maintained a morning discipline for over 60 years. In fact, the busier my days are, the more time I need to spend in quiet prayer. During those difficult years at Pilgrim Church, while I was defying my 'black dog' (Churchill's label for his depression) an hour would seem barely sufficient.

In spite of this, by the abundance of Divine grace, my ministry at Pilgrim was blessed. Please do not think I was a perpetual grump. If anything, depression sharpened my sense of social, political and personal incongruities. My sense of humour would smash its way through my personal nimbus strata and provide a bright moment for whatever group I happened to be in. I had brief times of creativity, and in those moments made jottings for what a few years later would become the three volumes of *Brief Prayers for Australians*.

One Sunday at Pilgrim Church, a stranger attended evening prayers. He was passing through Adelaide and wanted to meet and thank me for my *Australian Prayers* and *Australian Psalms*. That man was Ian Morris, a lay preacher in the Northern Territory and a ranger at Kakadu National Park. This affable guy said he would be delighted if we would visit and stay with him in his National Park quarters. He wryly commented that he could improve on the photography used in my first two books.

We took him up on the offer in 1985. With our loyal ageing Datsun 180B, plus two small tents and basic camping gear, Marie Joyce and I spent our annual leave exploring the Red Centre and then staying a week with Ian. The experience of encountering Kakadu National Park in the company of an informed nature lover like Ian Morris was mind blowing; as was the photographic library he had amassed. For the first time in some years, I would rate my 'mood level' as 5-8 out of a possible 10.

A bi-product of that visit was our joint publication: a coffee table book, *Kakadu Reflections,* featuring Ian's superb photography and my poems. It proved a hit with tourists and ended up in far corners of the world. A few years later, I was deeply moved to hear that the eminent Australian historian, Prof. Manning Clarke, as he was slowly dying, kept that book by his bedside.

Back at Pilgrim Church, my good and able colleague, Grant Dunning, accepted a call to the UCA church at Walkerville. Grant was succeeded at Pilgrim Church by the Rev. Michael Sawyer. Mike was a perpetual optimist; a wonderful counter-balance to my moods; he was an excellent administrator, a jovial pastor and a fluent off-the-cuff speaker. We formed, I believe, as good a two-person team as was possible in this earthly church where ministerial egos abound. We co-opted the Baptist psychiatrist, Dr. Max Bawden, to be our counsellor and relationship enabler, meeting once a month for a couple of fruitful hours.

Among the many pastors of other churches in the city, I relished the friendship of two in particular: Barry Hibberd, the minister at Central Baptist Church in Flinders Street and Ron Williams, the Anglican 'priest to the city'; very different characters but each robust, wise and caring men. To be for a time the chairperson of the Inner City Ministers' Fraternal was a special privilege for the still shy BDP.

At Ballarat in Victoria, Martin and Lynne became the doting parents of Claire, our first granddaughter, in August 1986. Later that year, Nancy and David left England and settled in Sunbury, Victoria. Shortly after, we first met our oldest grandchild, Benjamin, an eight-month-old bundle of energy.

In the winter of 1987, we took six weeks' long service leave, towing our caravan up to Cairns in northern Queensland, before working our way back to Sunbury for a most auspicious event: Christine was to marry Nigel Senior at the oldest surviving homestead in Victoria, a place quaintly named *Emu Bottom*. Marie Joyce and I respected, admired and loved Nigel. It was a mighty thrill for me to be able to perform the wedding ceremony for them.

During my time in Adelaide, I was 'sounded out' (in view to issuing a call) by a number of other major congregations in Australia. None seemed right for us. In 1988, I received a most persistent call from the more modest congregation at St. Andrew's Bendigo. After months of soul searching, we finally said "okay". I agreed to become the minister of St. Andrew's in July, the following year.

Life at Pilgrim had been both wonderful, and at times distressing, with numerous tensions, broken relationships, salvaged marriages, angry minorities, precious yet prickly parishioners and the tragic deaths of young members. But there were also tremendous moments of worship, fellowship, outreach and self-sacrifice by some remarkable Christian people. The gifted lay people were too numerous for me to dare to even begin to mention any names. Christmas and Easter were always busy, bountiful seasons with hordes of worshippers packing the church to overflow, leaving minsters (and a number of lay folk) utterly exhausted, yet also feeling privileged and profoundly blessed.

By the end of our nine years at Pilgrim Church, numerically the congregations had ceased to grow and became static. This phase coincided with the loss of a nearby, free, large parking area to commercial development. In light of our contemporary addiction to transport by private motor cars, I formed a theory that it is difficult to foster numerical growth without having a readily accessible parking space for vehicles. Churches that are sited in the centre of our larger cities will usually have to contend with this significant handicap.

Through those nine years as a minister with the people at Pilgrim, I gave it my best shot, focussing on the things I did best: pastor, enabler, liturgist, preacher and spiritual advisor. During the last seven years, I battled ceaselessly against the inner darkness of depressive illness. And throughout that time, those many choice carers within the church community cherished Marie and me, enabling us to continue to grow in faith, hope and love.

ST. ANDREW'S BENDIGO

We came to the rural city of Bendigo in bleak mid-winter. It was chilly as we arrived at about 5.30pm to be met by a patient, welcoming group who had underestimated the time it would take us to tow a caravan from South Australia.

The manse, spacious and comfortable, sat in the shadow of the beautiful St. Andrew's Church building. The first sub-zero night we spent in our van on the front lawn. Furniture arrived on the morrow. After some days of unpacking, (my definition of hell is eternally packing and unpacking) we spent time in Sunbury with our son and daughter-in-law while we looked at 'houses for sale'.

We had sold our home at Magill before we left Adelaide and wanted to invest the money in another house, just in case 'house prices went mad and outstripped inflation'. The setting of a modest house at 5 Laureate Close, overlooking an untidy, scrubby valley that was the proposed site for a small lake, won our hearts. We purchased it and were able to lease it to conscientious tenants. We thought we might never actually live there (we would prefer a house by the sea) but at least our savings were invested in the property market.

Then it was back to Bendigo for my induction and the uptake of pastoral responsibilities. The induction service was a moving event, the warmth of the people most heartening. A sad note was that even before the induction I was able to spend special times with Iain Floyd, one of the most able elders, who was in the final stages of dying with cancer.

St. Andrew's had a proud history. Up until 30 years ago, the congregation had been large. Then, with the general decline in church commitment within the Australian community, plus the leakage of members (sadly, encouraged by one perverse minister-emeritus) at the time of the formation of the Uniting Church, it had become numerically weaker.

There were two services each Sunday morning, an informal at 9.30am and a traditional at 11am, with a combined attendance of only about 100. Yet there was a group of high quality people who were still active, consisting of long-time members and more recent arrivals.

Marie and I soon came to appreciate the depth of commitment and personal value of gifted long-standing members such as Arthur and Enid Rogers, Merle Farrar, Peter Randall, Jean Bennett, Kath Dennis, Gwen McDonald, Alison

Floyd, Maisie Ross, Hugh and Phil Ward, Carol and Max Williams and the parish treasurer, Les Cockerel. Among newer members were outstanding folk like David Castles (the fine church organist) and his wife Lorraine, David and Jenny Shields, Bruce and Carolyn Johnson, Nancy Bomford and others. We were also blessed to have as members of our congregation the Lidgett family; the Rev. Bill Lidgett was the Presbytery Officer (a role rather like a one-term bishop) and his wife Claire was a tireless champion of young people.

For 25 years, a few key women had run a weekly 'Creative Living Program' in the hall. Each Monday they provided craft, music and painting classes for the lonely, elderly and the physically or mentally handicapped. The program always included lunch for 60-80 people, served in style at small, café-style tables. This was a remarkable commitment by that brand of faith that truly works! Marie found a niche in the kitchen as one of the ladies who prepared the soup for lunch.

One little matter irked me. Not only was my predecessor's name still in large letters on the St. Andrew's noticeboard when I was inducted, but it stayed there for six months. My requests to the Property Committee were noted but nothing happened. It was nine months before the penny dropped; the real decision-making at St. Andrew's happened by chatter-consensus among those wonderful ladies who ran 'Creative Living'. A word in their ear and before long, wallah! My name appeared on the notice board of St. Andrew's. I had found the real power-base of that congregation. And a very worthy one it was!

Within a few months of our arrival, we were to make a sad visit back to Pilgrim Church. My much-loved colleague and dear friend, Michael Sawyer, died suddenly from a heart attack. We hastily drove across to Adelaide, to give whatever support we could to Joan Sawyer and to share with the congregation in their shock and grief.

St. Andrew's was the only church in central Bendigo that still had their minister residing next door. Guess which minister it was (or his long-suffering wife) that both the professional cadgers and the genuine needy, found it easy to locate? The manse was fitted with three doorbells, each omitting a different buzz. One bell was for the minister's study, one was for the house, and a third was sited on the rear door. If the front door bell rang long and demandingly, it was sure to be a pro cadger. If the back door bell rang, it could be either a genuinely needy person or someone popping across from the church. Usually a short ring on the study bell meant it was genuine church business, including folk coming for pre-wedding interviews.

A parson can find himself doing seemingly contradictory things. In Glenorchy I pressed for separation, at Mt. Waverley I worked for a joining of congregations, at Essendon I encouraged one large parish, and finally at Bendigo I successfully sought an excision of St. Andrew's and Axedale from the northern churches. In all cases, I still think it was the wise path take *at that time.* The mission needs of the growing population at the northern end were different from those of St. Andrew's in the centre of the city.

My health was not the best. Although my Adelaide doctor had given me a clean sheet before I accepted the call to Bendigo, my old 'black dog' still stalked me. My refusal to bow to my illness meant that, piece by piece, other things started to go wrong physically.

My three-volume *Brief Prayers* hit the bookshops, as did a coffee table book, *Outback Reflections,* co-authored with Lutheran Aub Podlick, with photography by the renowned Jocelyn Burt.

Soon after followed a volume of imagined 'conversations' with the living Lord Jesus, bearing the title *The Boomerang Bender.* I winced when I first saw the cover and print style of the last item; it was ghastly. Purple and yellow? It seemed to Marie and me that this book could not possibly sell well. It didn't.

Winter was proving to be my Achilles heel, with repeated chest infections, bowel cramps and other ills. In 1991, we took six weeks' unpaid leave and camped at Bargara Beach in Queensland, but as I returned to the parish, my struggle against the 'black dog' was becoming more desperate.

After a succession of funerals, I commented to Marie that I should be able make it through to Christmas, just as long as no one else in the congregation died. The ever-positive, wonderful Carol Williams did just that; a sudden heart attack; no warning. I think I coped with the funeral rites competently, but Marie could see I was in a bad way. My dear wife spoke with the caring Nancy Bomford who quickly brought her psychiatrist husband John (a true pastor if ever I met one!) into the situation.

John was nonplussed at the medication that I had been put on in Adelaide. He 'dried me out' over two weeks and then prescribed something more appropriate. Improvement came within 10 days of taking the new medication; while driving out of town to lead worship at Axedale, for the first time in months I really saw the contours and colours of field and forest and rejoiced in them. My well-being rating (out of a possible high of 10) seemed to steady out at about 5-6 on my mood scale, but that was not enough for me to keep on top of my pastoral responsibilities, given the dicey state of my physical health.

In the New Year, John Bomford took definitive action. He referred me to the Victorian Synod Medical Board. After checking me out, one medical examiner said "You will retire immediately. Today." Two days later, I attended another consultation and that second examiner said, "I want you to terminate as from the conclusion of next Sunday." When I asked "After a few months rest, could I perhaps do some locum supply from time to time?" She shook her head and said "I strongly urge you not to. You have done enough damage to your system for one life time."

I almost complied but there were a few essentials to be cleaned up first, including some special pastoral visits that needed to be made. A fortnight later, in February, we said farewell to St. Andrew's. I still felt so ashamed of my "failure to finish the course" that I could not openly tell the dear folk at my farewell that endogenous depression was at the root of my poor health. I did, however, assure them that my health was in no way their fault, nor was any tension or problem within the congregation.

God was good. Not only had She given me a loving and pro-active psychiatrist (John Bomford) when I most desperately needed it, there was also an empty house waiting for us at Sunbury. When we rang the tenant to give her notice she said: "I am so glad you rang. Today I have been trying to pluck up courage to let you know that we wish move, as soon as possible, up-country to Nagambie."

Bruce and Marie renewing their vows on the occasion of
their 40th Wedding Anniversary, with Rev. Dean Ely,
St. Andrew's Uniting Church, Sunbury, 1995

Our Bonus Years

Sunbury 1992--

On the 5th March 1992, we packed up and moved into 5 Laureate Close, Sunbury, Victoria. Marie Joyce and I chuckled over the name of our new address: 'Laureate' sounded rather pretentious? Any hubris dissipated when we discovered that the streets in our region were named after famous racehorses that in earlier years had been trained at Sunbury.

I felt enormously relieved to be liberated from having to wear a 'public persona'. I felt as light as angels wings yet there was also a heavy sense of shame and deep loss. I had not gone the distance. No longer a person of clout. Asked to refrain for leading worship and preaching. Who was I now? How could I fulfil my ordination, which was, and still is, for life?

I threw myself into physical activity. Terraced the grounds at the back of the house and prepared garden beds. Dug up the front lawn and reseeded it. Constructed bookshelves and cupboards for my study. Enlarged, stained and polished a new kitchen dresser. Ordered fruit trees and grape vines to be planted in late winter. We engaged an architect to draw up plans for house alterations. On a cold, muddy May day, the builder commenced.

I had fully expected to now return to excellent, physical health. I was still receiving care from Dr. John Bomford and was feeling okay emotionally. However, evidently my exhausted body was saying to my mind: "Listen old mate. You have forced me to plod on relentlessly. Now it's my turn to be pampered."

A series of ailments (11 in all) some puzzling, others readily diagnosed, plagued me over the following months. With three of these aliments, 'specialist' medicos independently commented: "It seems you have X, or Y, or Z. It is usually only diagnosed in the extremely elderly." That told me something!

For me there followed tedious winter months of being partly bedridden, or hobbling on a walking stick, and painful episodes spent in hospital. There I witnessed for myself how overtaxed were the emergency facilities and the staff in our public hospitals. The frail and the elderly waiting on trolleys or in wheelchairs all night for attention. Scandalous. Stupid restrictions like many hours without being allowed a drink, "not until the doctor has assessed you". When finally assessed and admitted, receiving an urgent drip; "severe dehydration, I am afraid" said the attending nurse. There is truth in the comment from an older minister, "You need to be fit before you get admitted to hospital."

In August, the builders finished our house alterations. Our dear friend Ivan Wilson came to rescue my hessian-bagged fruit trees. He punched holes into the heavy clay soil and planted nine fruit trees and two grape vines. Just as well Ivan did not have a dicky heart!

By April 1993 my health had steadied. We planned what was to be the first of many winter migrations to sunny Queensland. By the providence of God, and the curiosity of Marie, we found Horseshoe Bay, Bowen, and the warm congregation at St. James' Uniting Church. The minister was Alf Dixon. Alf was a spiritual tonic. Week after week through prayer and the Word, he saturated us in the abundance of God's grace. I was liberated to commence creative writing again; maybe ministry was not a thing confined to yester-year?

Back home, I had drawn up a list of goals.

1/ Do all I could to cherish Marie Joyce as she deserves.

2/ Write daily and seek to improve the quality of my writing.

3/ Get over my hang-up about computers; learn the basics.

Meanwhile, while my *psyche, soma* and *persona* were untangling themselves, we were blessed with more beautiful grandchildren. To Ben and Claire were added Sarah, Alice, Rachel, Kate, Michael, and in 1995, Lachlan.

I hope I have met my first goal. Marie loves travel and especially revels in places by the sea. In 1994, we did our first extended, caravan tour around Australia; on the road for five months. Early the next year we also bought a cabin in a tourist park at Apollo Bay. Many beautiful hours have been spent there, cherishing each other.

The third goal was also reached. Thanks to the stubborn determination of our good friend Lyn Wilson (who knew nothing of my secret vow), followed by the encouragement of son David and son-in-law Nigel, I picked up the basics of using a PC. This proved most valuable for my future writing.

As to whether the second aspiration was achieved, I have no objective measuring stick. However, when in 1993 *Prayers for Aussie Kids,* and in 1996 *More Australian Psalms,* came off the presses at 'Openbook Publishers' in Adelaide, I might have taken that step up? I do consider some my best poetic writing is among the prayers and poems of the latter book.

(It needs to be mentioned that not all my creative efforts have been we rewarded with publication. No way! There have been three other substantial manuscripts, each representing at least six months' labour, that were rejected by publishers.)

Sightly enlarged editions of my first two poetic books were published in the year 2000 and 2002 respectively. And as if in a 'last hurrah', a new volume of prayers and poems, titled *Australians At Prayer,* was launched in 2004. I was sure it would be my 'swan song', my final published work.

During these bonus years, the internet became the focus of my ministry. Although I remain largely computer illiterate, in the late 1990s I felt called to use the web for ministry. Throughout our travels I had been made aware of the small army of lay people who each week front up and prepare to lead worship in rural churches across this wide continent and its surrounding islands. These folk are indeed the salt of the earth. I guessed how hard it must be after a busy working week in secular toil, to come up with fresh material for worship, so I decided to place on my web page some resources, based on the Revised Common Lectionary, which might perhaps assist lay leaders.

With the invaluable help of Nigel my son-in-law, over the next three years, prayers poems and sermons for each Sunday were provided. The word about my web page slowly spread and the result has been beyond expectations. Even though these days there are now dozens of other sites like mine, each month an average 12,000 people will choose to access my web page. Many of these are those Uniting Church lay preachers whom I first had in mind, and in other cases they are numerous ministers and priests of other denominations. A trickle of email quietly flows from ministers, priests, nuns and from lay folk, from Australia, New Zealand, USA, Canada, Southeast Asia, South Africa and the UK, and even a few from France, Germany and Switzerland.

The best joy of our bonus years has been to watch our grandchildren grow up from tiny tots into capable young women and men. They are all beautiful young adults, with so much love to share and in turn receive. What is more, they do share it widely.

That is not to say they do not have obstacles to face and conquer. One of our wonderful granddaughters seems to have inherited from my genes, one that predisposes towards depression. Depression struck her down in the wake of glandular fever. It has been a long haul for this dear young woman to accept the handicap, but she is now rising above it gloriously. Another has, it seems, received either from me, or from another side of her familial gene pool, the handicap of bipolar mood swings; she also is now defiantly coping with this burden. One grandson, who is much-gifted with both many talents plus some esoteric muscle-wasting condition, is taking a long, long time to select from his gifts and commence developing a few to the full.

Some of our grandchildren are active Christians, others are agnostic. Yet they each insist on being loving persons and hence are themselves lovable. We are proud to be known as their 'Grandma Marie and Grandad Bruce'. If they are a sample of the next generation, then by the grace of God the world is in good hands.

In matters of health we continue to have our ups and downs. In December 2000, Marie Joyce was diagnosed with a bone-marrow blood disorder. She required a daily oral intake of a 'mild' chemo (relatively speaking) and needs regular venesections. Three years after, I was diagnosed with the same condition and have received the same treatment. We've coped well with the disorder and at present we both appear to be in some kind of remission.

More recently, in 2010, I was found to be suffering also from Parkinson's Disease. The prospect of being increasingly disabled does not thrill me, but after the initial shock, I am embracing P.D. as a way of becoming more and more dependent on nothing but the grace of God in our Lord Jesus Christ. So far, medication is helping. Although I have difficulty swallowing, my balance is shot to pieces, handwriting has gone defunct, speech is getting harder, even using the keyboard of a PC has become a tedious 'hunt-and-peck method', I do manage some creative writing.

Significant assistance has come from two quarters. First, from the helpfulness of Helen Hall, a lovely member of our St. Andrew's congregation in Sunbury, who in an honorary capacity uses her secretarial expertise to unscramble my literary mess-ups. Secondly, the advent of improved 'speech recognition software' has enabled me to continue to produce some significant writing.

The year 2012 saw the arrival of a book for older children, titled *My Best Mate*. This has largely come about through the generosity of a dear, special American friend, Mary Catharine Nelson, of *Ideas into Books*® Westview publishers. She has encouraged me to keep writing. Another book, *Day by Day, Brief Prayers for Busy People,* is likely to be available, both in Australia and in the USA this year, 2014.

In whatever time we have left, Marie I will cherish each other day by day. We remain proud of the kind of persons our three, now aging, offspring are still becoming. We deeply value the love, care and wisdom of our two daughters-in-law Nancy and Lynne, and of our one son-in-law Nigel. And, as the reader will have gathered, we follow with daily love and prayer the activities of the eight grandchildren and their respective partners.

I'd like to finish this account with one of my better moments. It was at Pilgrim Church, Adelaide, one Sunday after a 7 o'clock service of Evening Prayers, that a stranger shook my hand and with a wry grin commented: *"For years I have treasured your writing, Bruce. You've helped me more times than I can count. Tonight I have travelled a considerable distance in order to meet with you. I must say it has been a major disappointment! You are not the colossus I had built you up to be. You are just an just ordinary bloke like the rest of us."*

"Exactly! Thank God," I exclaimed, with a grin from ear to ear. We chuckled together and walked through into the church lounge to enjoy supper.

I am regularly confounded. The creativity of the Sisterly Spirit has been able to use my limited talents beyond all rational explanation, even well into old age. I am filled with gratitude and wonder at such mercy heaped upon mercy, full and overflowing. Grace; that is the bottom line.

What else is there to say?

AFTERWORD

Hello Bruce.

I am the American daughter of an Australian who has been living in the U.S. for almost 70 years. For quite some time I've been enjoying your worship materials, and for some reason it only tonight occurred to me that if your prayers are out of print, I could take care of that for you. (Besides being a part-time pastor, I've somehow over the years become a book publisher as well.)

Normally I get paid to turn people's materials into books (either print or e-books), but for purely selfish reasons I'd like to volunteer to make your worship materials available at no charge, if you would like that. Goodness knows, I've made use of your services enough times that it would be only fair for me to make my 'services' available to you. You can check out my website at www.publishedbywestview.com if you would like to know more about my company.

I normally print through a company known as Lightning Source (a subsidiary of Ingram), but I believe they now print in Australia as well as the U.S. – regardless, e-books are available worldwide. If you are interested, just let me know.

Thanks!

Mary Catharine Nelson

♯

Hi Mary,

What a wonderful surprise! Your most generous offer has left me gob-smacked! I will gladly accept. Your email came after a week in which I had been praying and mulling over the question: "What next has the Holy Friend in store for me? Have I reached a stage of ageing (and declining health) where I must be content with just being instead of doing things within the ongoing ministry of Christ Jesus? Have I reached my use-by date?"

As I opened my mailbox this morning, I paused and prayed for grace to handle well anything that might be in it. Oddly there was only one email (none of the usual guff to sort out and delete) awaiting me. Yours, Mary. I had the answer to my mulling and praying.

The thought of re-publishing some of my outpourings had not seemed possible. Most of the Christian publishers in Australia have gone to the wall in the last few years. The market for Christian books has shrunk drastically in recent decades in this country. That market has always been small. This has never been a religious nation, but a rampant secularism has eaten deeply into last two generations of Aussies, making that market even smaller. Living on a modest retirement pension, I could not afford to self-publish. Beside I am a creative soul, not organised and efficient enough to handle self-publishing.

A warning. You need to know that I can only work slowly these days. The creeping effects of Parkinson's Disease has damaged my manual dexterity, limiting my typing to a tedious one-finger performance. But if you are still game to take me on, I am ready to give it a go.

Your unexpected communication is to me yet another example of the free, overflowing 'grace upon grace' from the full store of God in Christ Jesus: that holy abundance which has marked every step of my pilgrimage.

Thank you, Mary.
Bruce Prewer

Hi wonderful Mary!

The package of books arrived safely today, just one hour ago. It has engendered a certain amount of excitement in the hearts of two elderly young people. Marie Joyce is already reading *My Best Mate*. She has of course read it before, but has now mumbled something about "It's amazing how much smarter this seems now this is published as a book."

I will get around to reading it again sometime. It's still too close to all the hassle of finally getting it ready for publication to be appreciated by me, yet. But it is good to see it in print at last. I like what you have done with the covers and with the additional notes, et cetera. Having been asked to write it by my then publisher about 12 years ago, and then having the plug pulled when they went broke, I was left a little bereft. It then became to me almost like a stillborn child. But now, like a surrogate mother, you, wonderful Mary, have come along. And now here are some thoughts I set down a dozen years ago. From the bottom of my heart I thank you and the God of all grace who has linked us to you as a dear friend.

What I am really interested at this very moment is the other four books you sent me. I have only briefly glanced at your two books Mary, but I'm already emotionally involved in your tribulations. You seem to have been to the deepest Sheol and back.

The other two publications by author Lane Denson, also appear to be great stuff! Already I have noted him referring to God as SHE. I am immediately won over and look forward to using them as a part of my daily quiet time over the next couple of months.

The post is certainly sluggish around Christmas time; our Australian postal services become markedly delinquent in the post-Christmas hangover. Another parcel from a friend in Tasmania, our neighbouring state, which was posted the same time as yours, only arrived are few days ago.

You will certainly hear from me again soon Mary. Right now I just had to explode with the news that your parcel had arrived safely.

Much love,
Bruce and Marie Joyce Prewer

♪

Dear Mary,

Yesterday I completed reading *Job of Arc*. But I have not finished thinking about it, not by a long shot! You wondered if I might find it too heavy going and suggested that if so, I could skip to the nice bits in the Implications section. Not on your cotton-pickin life! It was a painful story to read but the pastor in me found it utterly compelling, so much so that the last unit of the book left me feeling a bit ho-hum... after the tension of the major part of your account. In fact I intend to read that last section again to get maximum blessing from it.

I have journeyed profoundly with you from when you were a seven-year-old child reading Charles Dickens, to the terrible abuses you suffered during your childhood, to your first ill-fated marriages, to the unwillingness of your mother to hear you (sadly, so typical) throughout your desecrated early years, through to the courage that lead you to adopt the boys and foster the girls, to your hope that seemed to be fulfilled with Jack, your heartbreak with Liberty, and then to the calamitous trashing of your self image as you got some of the truth out of Jack. Yet you were still hanging in there!

I wept with you in your personal Garden of Gethsemane; sensed your torment over the reaction of the church where you belonged for so long, marvelled at your attempt to still care for Jack, was awed by your unconditional commitment to troubled kids, felt frustrated and then damn angry by the obdurate state welfare agencies, was shattered by the 'cruellest blow of all', sensed the dark night of your depression as you came within an inch of taking your life, was so proud when Connor finally received his hard-won certificate, and breathed one enormous sigh of relief when you began to see a tiny bit of light at the end of your dark tunnel.

And then, just a few years later, you email an aged minister in Australia offering to publish his neglected worship resources. Wow! WOW! WOW!

Mary Mary quite contrary, you are one mighty Christ-like woman! I mean it! You are truly one of the most remarkable faith survivors I have ever encountered.

You are one hell-ava example (pardon the mixed metaphor) of the grace of the Goddess redemptively at work in and through your many sufferings. Isaiah 53 comes alive in your saga. Just substitute 'she' for 'he' and you will see (I hope) the connection.

Thank you for sending us this inimitable document, *Job of Arc*, and for letting us know it is autobiographical. That in itself takes much courage. And lady, you do have courage + + + !

Marie Joyce and I feel honoured to have read and travailed through your story. We would be exceedingly proud if you were our daughter.

With much love and great respect!
Bruce

Hi Mary,

I'm wondering when the copies of *My Best Mate*, the Australian edition without the glossary, will be available from the Australian branch of your printers? I have a number of people interested in getting a copy.

Also, when the copies are available from it, I would like to place some in Australian bookshops and distribution agents. Do you see any problem with that?

I am now slowly re-reading, and pondering, the last sections of *Job of Arc*. Your ruminations no longer seem to be 'ho-hum'. Like you, I wrestle with the issue of the apparent unfairness of life; the key theme of the book which Job so magnificently struggles with. I agree with those Old Testament scholars who reckon the text originally finished at Chap 42, V 9. For me, one of the most powerful parts of the whole story comes in verses 7 to 9.

To have Yahweh rebuke one of Job's tormentors, Eliphaz the Temanite, "My wrath is kindled against you and against your two friends; for you have not spoken of me what is right, as my servant Job has" it is to me the climax of the account. The message from God is loud and clear: Job was right in complaining about the unfairness of life. His tormentors were wrong in trying to find a slick and pious answer to the dilemma of suffering and injustice. Job called it as it really was. The question is valid and cannot be put aside with a few religious clichés.

By the way, in my childhood I also disliked the story of Job, but for different reasons. The tiny little country weatherboard hall where I used to go to church, was, three Sundays out of four, served by a lay preacher. One of them, a most ponderous character called Mr. Buck, always had his Children's Address on the boring topic of 'the temptations of Job'. Every time he was rostered to be the preacher, my sister and I prepared for the worst. And we always got it! He was really the most dull prattler who ever came to our church; but at least boredom was preferable to some of the hellfire preachers we had to suffer on other Sundays. But that is another story. How I ended up as a believer defies rational explanation!

Enough. Love,
Bruce

Hi Mary,

It seems ages ago that I asked you for some photos of your family and promised to send some of mine. With your usual efficiency, you quickly responded with your photos, in which MJ found a lot of pleasure. It is great to get some faces on people that you had been mentioning.

My response has been much more sluggish. Apologies. I asked my daughter-in-law Lynne, who is the star photographer in our clan, but she has been a little tardy. So finally I have tried to get some together from my own photos and files.

The first photo is of our eldest son David and his family: From left to right they are, Michael 20, Benjamin 27, Sarah 25, Rachel 23, Nancy and David. Second photo is of our second son Martin and his lot: Claire 26, Lynne, Martin and Alice 23.

Third (three photos) our daughter Christine and her husband Nigel, Kate 21 and Lachlan 18. (The photo of Kate shows her with a rare, tiny, Leadbeater possum which had been considered extinct in the Victorian Alps. It was a most exciting discovery by Kate and the small group of researchers from her university.)

Above: Michael, Benjamin, Sarah, Rachel, Nancy, David
Below: Claire, Lynne, Martin, Alice

Christine and Nigel   Kate   Lachlan

The rest of the photos include some informal ones, from Christmas and a birthday party, a few of Marie Joyce and me and some from the house where we lived on the outskirts of the town Sunbury for 20 years until our recent shift into a town unit, forced by my failing health.

Bruce and Marie Joyce with Michael

Above: family camp – Sarah, Andy, Max

Below: Martin, David, Bruce

Above and below: Bruce and Marie

Above: David, Sarah, Ben, Bruce

Below: Marie, Rachel, Nancy

Above: MJP in the outback

Below: BDP at Outback Gorge

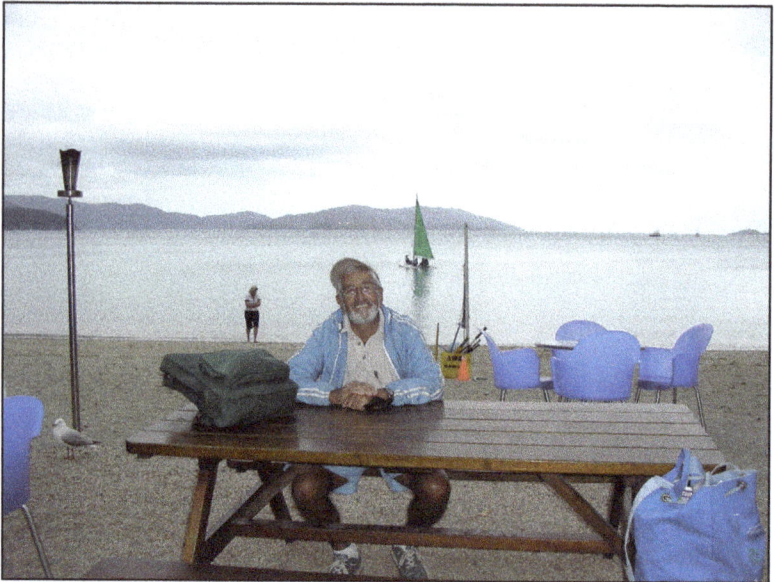

Above: relaxing on holiday

Below: Horseshoe Bay, Bowen

Above and below: Kata Tjuta (the Olgas)

Above: with one of the locals

Below: Tennant Creek area (tribute to Bill Allen)

Above: King Island with Nancy and David

Below: King Parrot, Apollo Bay

Above: MJP with English cousin Marie

Below: BDP and MJP

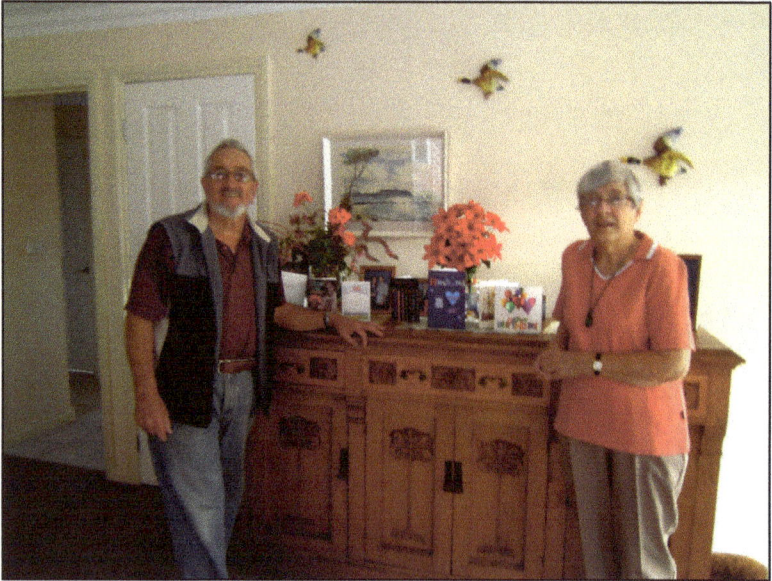

Very sad when we had to leave our 'home among the gum trees' beside the lake; it provided me with constant inspiration for writing. Yet we have made the adjustment better than we thought we could, and native birds still come to a birdbath outside the living room window.

Cockatoos enjoying the birdbath

I hope you enjoy getting names to the faces of our family and much as we have with yours.

May the joy of the Holy Friend continue to be yours, Mary.

Bruce P.

A couple of explanations:

Three of the pictures are from three years ago, when Marie made her first return visit to a small island to the north of Australia where she lived for the first five years of her life. Her parents were on a mission station on Goulburn Island, about 250 miles north-east of Darwin. It was quite an emotional journey for her. With her sister Jean, we chartered a small plane and stayed next door to the mission house of her childhood for two nights. One photo shows her and Jean showing photos to the oldest inhabitant in the community.

The chartered plane

MJP's first home

Oldest survivor, with Marie and Jean, Goulburn Island

One of the other photos is of our granddaughter Rachel, who, with some other young people from her church, set up a refugee type camp on the Village Green and they lived on rice and water for three days. This was a great witness to the community of the predicament facing refugees around the world. We were very proud of her.

Rachel and the Homeless Project

Love you MCN.
Bruce and Marie

Dear Mary,

You asked whether it was tough to leave our house by the lakeside It was. Very. Yet at that time it was also a big relief. I could not bear to see our home and surrounds fall into ruin.

Things have worked out much better than we had anticipated. Our health has steadied significantly. We love our cosy, new unit, which is sited in the 'old' part of Sunbury, in a tree-lined street. We have 'home help' that comes once a fortnight to clean and vacuum our quarters. My study-room is cramped and overflowing, but at least I do have my own den in which to be creative.

You have been very frank about your personal life. Maybe we should tell you a little about ours.

Marie Joyce is reticent about writing her life story, so I will go ahead right now and give you a précis of her first 18 years.

Marie had a fascinating childhood. Her first six years were spent among the aboriginal people of Warruwi, which is an island situated about 250 miles north-east of Darwin.

Her father, the Rev. George Goldsmith, was originally a boilermaker from Lancashire in England, Her mother, Jessie Osler, came from a farm in Victoria; she broke free from her family's constricting expectations, took herself off to Melbourne and qualified as a Triple Certificated Nurse. George and Jess offered to go to the tropics as missionaries when the wife of their predecessor took ill. They served there for seven years, George as missionary-pastor and Jess as the mission's nurse. It was a busy yet lonely life for the two 'whities'.

A supply lugger served the island only five times each year. Mail and food, and animated conversation with the white crew, were eagerly awaited whenever the lugger anchored in the bay.

Marie Joyce enjoyed an idyllic childhood, running free with her black playmates, getting into pranks and swimming in the tropical seas. She picked up the native language quickly, and for most of the time was the translator for her mum and dad. Her sister Jean was born (in Darwin) during the time they lived at Warruwi.

After a seven-year term, George took his family by steamship via the Suez to introduce them to his parents in Blackburn, England. To help pay their passage back to Australia, they ministered in the East End slums of London for a year, before saying a final goodbye to his parents and his only brother and sailing via the Panama Canal and the Pacific back to Australia.

Marie and Jean loved ship life and soon became seasoned little sailors. With their mother laid up with morning sickness, the two girls virtually had a free run of ship. Although her formal education was rather sketchy, with big gaps that still at times frustrate her, by the time Marie Joyce was eight years old, her life experience was extensive. Although she was too self-effacing to realise it, she was in fact quite a sophisticated little miss.

Soon after returning to Victoria, Jess travailed and brought forth a son, Ronald. Subsequently George was appointed to two Methodist parishes in Victoria, first to the inland wine-growing region of Rutherglen, and later to the seaside resort of Queenscliff. He was also a chaplain during the Second World War. After Queenscliff, he was a sent to a church in Hobart, Tasmania, and after just three years was 'promoted' to the Invermay Methodist Church in Launceston and to the position of 'State Secretary for Overseas Missions'.

Meanwhile, Marie was a student boarder at the very large and influential Methodist Ladies College, Melbourne. There, she and two mates, both also being ministers' daughters, engaged in many escapades. On leaving school, being a year too young to commence nurse training, she rejoined her family in Hobart and worked in a pharmacy for a year. The following year, 1949, was a momentous one for her: she turned 18, commenced nursing in Launceston, and met a shy but courteous young fellow named Bruce Prewer, who had never travelled outside of his small island state, Tasmania!

That's about all for now about Marie Joyce. Not being so backward these days, I had previously written a brief bio of the most significant events of my early years – see attachment (the major portion of this book). If you prove able to stomach this amount of detail without serious indigestion, I will later email you a potted bio of our lives for the last 60 plus years.

Good hunting, Mary.

Love you.

Bruce Prewer

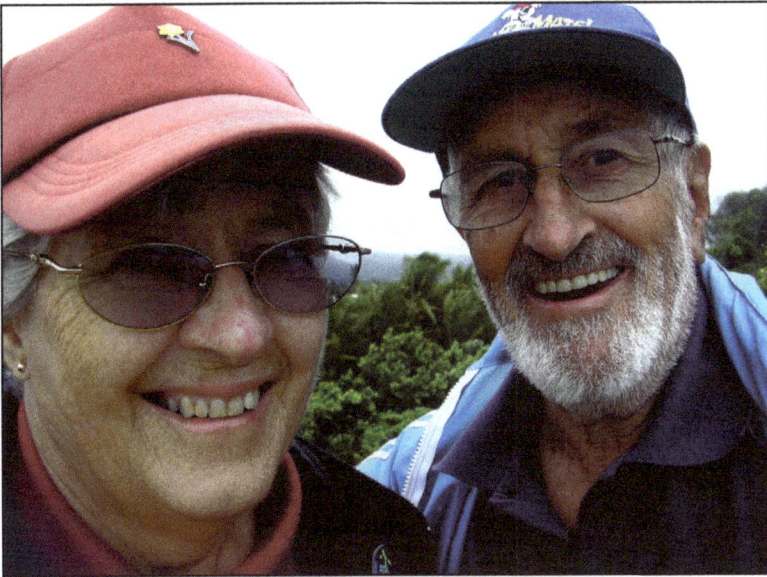

Pleased I finally made it through with the first few photos. A second batch is now attached. They show a bit of our old home's setting at 5 Laureate Close, and our present one at 3/66 Station Street.

From the opposite shore – our 'home among the gum trees'

Early morning

Evening

Early summer morning

Lachlan at our haven

It was an emotional wrench to move from our retirement home. We can understand how attached you are dear Mary, to your hard-won home in the woods. The 16 years we lived at Laureate Close was the longest time, by 9 years, that either of us had spent living anywhere. I have a strong hunch that the grace-full She-He-It (whom I refer to as the Holy Friend) had a finger in the circumstances that allowed us to retire there.

We added the solarium after we had settled in that spot. Most of my creative writing was done early while sitting in the morning sunshine looking through those wide windows.

A variety of waterbirds frequented the small lake, hundreds of corellas parked at night in the gum trees, and in the early mornings, a few big kangaroos would come down to the water's edge to drink, while magpies sat on the side fence many times and sang with their distinctive mellow warbling.

Above: from our solarium

Below: from the lakeside

Ibis and spoonbill

I may be an incurable romantic, but I treasured the arrival of two visitors while we lived there. One evening, at a time when I was feeling very down in health and spirits, there came a gentle rapping at the back door. On investigating, I found two native ducklings, aged about six weeks, tapping at the glass and expecting to be admitted.

They flopped over the doorstep and made themselves at home in our solarium. We fed them and gave them a small cardboard box, lined with an old cardigan, in which they could settle for the night. We enjoyed their company for some days, before they up and waddled off down our driveway and across to the lake. Whatever induced them to temporarily put aside their native shyness and give us the blessing of their company, I can only speculate, but these two little angels gave me some good cheer at the very time I badly needed it.

Two angels

So, dear Mary, selling our haven was indeed difficult. But for everything there is an opportune time. We did the right thing by moving into this unit. My health was very dicey at that time, and both my haematologist and I were unsure whether I would make it beyond six months. I could no longer cope with keeping the garden and house in good order.

Our new, unit-home is just two blocks away from doctor, pharmacist, supermarket and our church. It is also only a 15-minute walk to the train station. We have grown to truly enjoy our new setting and feel very content here.

Unit 3, 66 Station Street

Visitors at the Unit

Tiny garden

Back courtyard

The birdbath came with us and has a succession of honeyeaters, blackbirds, miners, sparrows, doves, and the occasional black crow, that splash around in it. Also, there are some lovely walks we can take from where we now live; each day we try to do between three and five kilometres.

Turtledoves at the birdbath

Speaking of angels, MJP has just tapped me on the shoulder reminding me that it is time for our morning walk.

Go well Mary, and continue to delight in your house in the woods.

Much love,

Bruce   XXXXXOOOOO

Lovebirds in their natural habitat